The BitterSweet World of
CHOCOLATE

The BitterSweet World of
CHOCOLATE

Troth Wells & Nikki van der Gaag

ni

THE BITTERSWEET WORLD OF CHOCOLATE

First published in the UK in 2006 by
New Internationalist™ Publications Ltd
55 Rectory Road
Oxford OX4 1BW, UK
www.newint.org
New Internationalist is a registered trade mark.

Front and back cover images, and all recipe photography © Kam & Co, Denmark.
email: studiet@kam.dk
Other back cover images: Boy in Ghana © Kim Naylor/Day Chocolate; Collins Adu Gyebi
© Karen Robinson/Day Chocolate.
© all other photographs rests with the individual photographers/agencies.

Text © Troth Wells and Nikki van der Gaag 2006.

Design by Alan Hughes and Andrew Kokotka/New Internationalist.

Printed on recycled paper in China by C&C Offset Printing Co. Ltd., who hold environmental accreditation ISO 14001.

British Library Cataloguing-in-Publication Data.
A catalogue record for this book is available from the British Library.
Library of Congress Cataloguing-in-Publication Data.
A catalogue for this book is available from the Library of Congress.

ISBN 10 - 1904456251
ISBN 13 - 9781904456254

Acknowledgements
Many thanks to the Day Chocolate Company (www.divinechocolate.com) for input and resources;
and also to William Beinart for his advice, and help with testing the recipes.

Contents

Foreword

MOST COCOA FARMERS have never eaten chocolate. Many don't even know that the cocoa they grow becomes this delicious treat that people all over the world are so fond of! For them cocoa is the crop they tend, and carefully ferment and dry year in and year out, and for which they hope they will be paid enough to live on. The rest of the story of cocoa is a mystery to them.

The cocoa farmers I work with at the Kuapa Kokoo co-operative in Ghana are an exception. They know how much their crop is valued by the outside world – and for the cocoa that is sold to the fair-trade market, that value is recognised by a fair price. Even more exceptionally the members of this co-operative own a chocolate company, which is a joy, and makes the cocoa farmers very proud. They could never have imagined they would own a third of a company in London – The Day Chocolate Company. They can share in the success of Day's 'Divine' and 'Dubble' fair-trade chocolate in the UK, and feel proud to ensure that all the cocoa they sell lives up to their motto 'the best of the best' or 'pa pa paa!' in our language.

I look forward to the day when a much larger percentage of what we and other small-scale poor peasant farmers around the world grow is sold for a fair price, giving people a sustainable income and the dignity that comes with it. This will happen because people will read books like this. More consumers will want it, governments will support it and ultimately companies will see it is right. At the end of the day, we all have to go shopping – and fair trade is just shopping with a heart!

KAREN ROBINSON / DAY CHOCOLATE

Mr Kwabena Ohemeng-Tinyase
Managing Director, Kuapa Kokoo Ltd
Ghana

The BitterSweet World of Chocolate

'There is a kind of alchemy in the transformation of base chocolate into this wise fool's gold, a layman's magic which even my mother might have relished. As I work I clear my mind, breathing deeply...The mingled scents of chocolate, vanilla, heated copper and cinnamon are intoxicating, powerfully suggestive...This is how I travel now, as the Aztecs did in their sacred rituals. Mexico, Venezuela, Colombia. The court of Montezuma, Cortez and Columbus. The food of the gods, bubbling and frothing in ceremonial goblets. The bitter elixir of life.'

JOANNE HARRIS *Chocolat*

POP A CHOCOLATE into your mouth. Let it melt slowly on your tongue. Savor its rich sweet taste. And then sit back and enjoy the story of chocolate. It has all the elements of the best tales: sacrifice and joy, philanthropy and exploitation, the darkness of slavery and the kindness of the human heart. Chocolate has always given pleasure, but it has also had its bitter undertones.

The story begins deep in the forests of America, many thousands of years ago, where great civilizations used the cocoa bean as money

Cocoa tree in Penang, Malaysia.

and worshipped the cocoa tree. The Mayans called it 'God Food'. The Aztecs used their bitter drink to sustain those whose hearts failed while being sacrificed to the gods. Their Spanish conquerors, though repelled at first by its bitter taste, found that a draught of chocolate could sustain them for a whole day's hard marching.

The tale continues across the oceans, from the New World to the Old. The secret of chocolate, blended with sugar and spices, remained with Spanish monks and princes for 100 years until it gradually spread to other countries. Fuelled by their desire for its delicious taste, the rulers of Europe established plantations in countries of the Equator, where the tree thrives. They brought slaves to pick the crop under the burning sun, and ships to bring it back home.

In the slums of their cities, men and women of good heart wanted to build a better world, free from drunkenness and violence, where people could live comfortably and in peace with their children. The new emperors of chocolate, often from poor families themselves, built their empires on the belief that their workers should be rewarded for their labors and their loyalty. They believed too that chocolate could replace the alcohol that they saw as such a destructive force in their society.

But chocolate has always been unequal fare. Cocoa is grown in poor countries by those who have never tasted chocolate and eaten by those in rich countries who have never known what it is like to be really poor. For the 10 million families in the South who depend on it for a living, the price of cocoa on the world market rides a roller-coaster. It is a vulnerable crop, difficult to grow and hard to harvest. And yet huge profits are made by the big multinational companies who process, market and sell chocolate, its end product.

The rich world, it seems, cannot do without the food of the gods. We eat 79 per cent of all chocolate. Look around you on a bus or in a crowded street and there is likely to be more than one person munching on a chocolate bar. The Swiss, at 22 pounds or 10 kilos per person per year, eat the most; in the United Kingdom it is over 17 pounds (nearly 8 kg), in Australia 13 (5.8 kg), in the United States nearly 12 (5.4 kg). Chocolate is also increasingly popular in countries like China and Japan where people do not traditionally have a sweet tooth.

So what is the secret of this popularity? 'Hershey's chocolate makes people happy,' says the current website for the American giant. Chocolate has been associated with love and sex since the Aztec emperor Montezuma used it as an aphrodisiac. There have long been extravagant claims about its health-giving properties. Chocolate, it seems, can cheer the fainthearted, comfort the afflicted – and boost your love life.

But increasingly we also want to eat our chocolate (and other foods) with a good conscience. Everywhere in the rich world, people are putting their money where their mouths are and buying chocolate that does not exploit other people. Sophi Tranchell, Managing Director of the Day Chocolate Company which produces fairly traded chocolate, says: 'If more people bought in a discerning way, giving priority to the fact that producers got a fair price, it would make a real difference.' The story of chocolate could end happily ever after. It is up to you, the consumer. So lick your fingers as you stir in these recipes. Enjoy, explore, taste – and feel good about it. ■

OPPOSITE PAGE: TROTH WELLS

A passion for chocolate

'WHEN I DIE,' I said to my friend, 'I'm not going to be embalmed, I'm going to be dipped.' 'Milk or bittersweet?' was her immediate concern. This is the rhetorical response of one chocolate addict to another. We both knew the answer: 'Bittersweet'.

ADRIENNE MARCUS *THE CHOCOLATE BIBLE.*

Chili con carne with chocolate

A classic dish, and the cocoa gives it a wonderful rich note. 'We buy our cocoa from Kuapa Kokoo in Ghana, a farmers' co-operative that part owns the company and prides itself on the quality of its beans,' says fair-trade Day Chocolate Company. 'The beans are grown in the shade of the rainforest, carefully fermented and dried for a week in the sun, creating the full, rich chocolatiness.'

Serves 6-8
Preparation: 20 minutes
Cooking: 45 minutes

INGREDIENTS

1½ pounds / 750 g ground/minced beef

1 can red kidney beans, drained (retain liquid)

1 green bell pepper, chopped

2 onions, chopped

4 cloves garlic, crushed

2 tablespoons tomato purée

1 tablespoon tomato catsup/ketchup

1 teaspoon chili powder

2 tablespoons cocoa

2 teaspoons ground cumin

1 teaspoon dried oregano

¼ teaspoon ground cloves

⅛ teaspoon nutmeg

¼ teaspoon allspice

1 tablespoon vinegar

2 teaspoons sugar+

½ cup / 120 ml water or kidney beans liquid

oil

salt

+optional

1 To start, heat the oil in a large saucepan and when it is hot, sauté the onions until they are golden and soft; remove from the pan.

2 Now put the beef into the hot oil and seal it so that it is brown on all sides, adding the garlic.

3 Add the kidney beans, green pepper, tomato purée and ketchup, chili, cocoa, cumin, oregano, cloves, nutmeg, allspice, vinegar, sugar (if using) and liquid. Bring to the boil and then reduce heat and simmer for 45 minutes. Stir from time to time, and add more liquid if required to prevent catching.

4 Season and adjust flavorings before serving with sour cream or yogurt and rice.

Spanish roast with chocolate

Good flavors with a rich sauce from the chocolate. The Fairtrade Labelling Organization (FLO) has cocoa-producing partners in Costa Rica, Nicaragua, Belize, Dominican Republic, Bolivia, Peru, Cameroon, Côte d'Ivoire and Ghana.

Serves 6-8
Preparation: 10 minutes
Cooking: 2½-3 hours

INGREDIENTS

4-pound/2-kg beef roast

3-4 onions, sliced in rings

6 cloves

1 tablespoon vinegar

1 bay leaf

1 teaspoon cinnamon

2 tablespoons catsup/ketchup

2 ounces / 50 g dark chocolate*
  broken into pieces

a little flour

2 cups water

oil

salt and pepper

* Cooking or baker's chocolate. Use sweet, semisweet or unsweetened according to your preference. Semisweet or bittersweet is fine for most dishes.

1 Use a little flour and dust the roast on all sides. Then heat some oil in a large pan with a lid and brown the meat on all sides, stirring from time to time. If the flour begins to catch, add a little water and stir to mix. Remove the roast and set aside.

2 Line the base of the pan with the onion rings, adding salt and pepper. Put the roast on top of the onion rings and then add the cloves, vinegar, bay leaf, cinnamon, ketchup and water.

3 Cover the pan and bring to the boil. Then reduce the heat and simmer gently for 2-2½ hours until the meat is tender.

4 Add the chocolate and stir it around the roast to melt and blend well, while the dish cooks gently for a further 5-10 minutes.

CHOCOLATE. *The word alone can make your mouth water. No other food produces such a range of emotions. The distinctive aroma, the smooth texture, the sweet taste cannot be found in combination anywhere else. Chocolate has over 400 distinct smells – the rose has only fourteen and the onion just six or seven.*

Aztec attraction

MARY EVANS PICTURE LIBRARY

Aztecs preparing a cup of chocolate, Mexico.

THE 16TH CENTURY Aztec Emperor Montezuma was reputed to believe that chocolate was an aphrodisiac. The link between chocolate and sex continued down the centuries. It was favored by Casanova (1725-98), who called it 'the elixir of love' and drank it instead of champagne. In France, the Marquis de Sade (1740-1814) was supposed to have added chocolate to the stimulants served at a dinner party:

'The marquis had mixed with the dessert a profusion of chocolate, flavored with vanilla, which was found delicious, and of which everybody freely partook. All at once the guests, both men and women, were seized by a burning sensation of lustful ardor; the cavaliers attacked the ladies without any concealment.' 'I wish for a chocolate cake so dense,' he once wrote his wife from one of his stints in jail, 'that it is black, like the devil's ass is blackened by smoke.'

But the link with love also meant that the Church, in particular, disapproved. In 1624, author Joan Roach devoted a whole book to its condemnation, referring to it with puritanical disapproval as a 'violent inflamer of the passions'. The poet James Wadsworth had this provocative stanza about chocolate in one of his poems:

> *Twill make Old women Young and Fresh;*
> *Create New Motions of the Flesh;*
> *And Cause them long for you know what;*
> *If they but taste of chocolate.*

The language of chocolate

LINGUISTS BELIEVE THAT the origin of the word 'cacao' is a Mixe-Zoquean word (perhaps from *kakawa*) that predates the Mayans. Nahuatl was the most common indigenous language in South America. Its word for chocolate is *cachuatl*. The Mayans called their Tree *Cacahuaquchtl*. But the Spanish conquistadors found the 'l' difficult to pronounce and replaced it with an 'e'. There was also confusion with the word 'coco' which was what the Europeans called the coconut. Coco was a Portuguese word meaning a 'head with a smile'. When cacao made its debut in Britain, the vagaries of English spelling and pronunciation led the poor 16th century Brits to scramble words to make a different name.

Another theory is that the word chocolate was inspired by the sound the water made when stirred into a cup of chocolate that would then bubble 'choco, choco, choco'. And finally, because the Spanish word for excrement is *caca*, it is said the word for the divine drink was changed so that it did not sound too similar.

Chocolate & zucchini/ courgette chili

Yellow or green zucchini/courgettes absorb the flavors of the chili well. The dish can also be made with 1-2 cans of cooked beans such as red kidney beans.

You can use the mix to serve with rice, such as fairly traded supplies from Agrocel's 20 small, family farms in Haryana state in India. As well as a better price, farmers get free technical services from Agrocel and are encouraged to develop sustainable agriculture.

Serves 4-6
Preparation: 20 minutes
Cooking: 40-50 minutes

INGREDIENTS

1 pound / 450 g ground/minced beef

2 zucchini/courgettes, chopped

1 onion, chopped

1 can tomatoes, chopped

1 cup / 240 ml beer or chicken broth

1 teaspoon cumin

½ teaspoon cinnamon

1 clove

2 teaspoons cocoa

1-2 cloves garlic, crushed

¼-½ teaspoon cayenne pepper

cheddar cheese, grated

oil

salt and pepper

Heat oven to 350°F/180°C/Gas 4

1 Sauté the onion in a little oil and add the beef to brown.

2 Now add the zucchini/courgettes and cook gently until they are soft.

3 Add the tomatoes with their liquid as well as the beer or broth.

4 Now add the cumin, cinnamon, clove, cocoa, garlic and cayenne pepper. Season, and then cover and simmer for 20 minutes. If you prefer it thicker, uncover the pan and boil to reduce the liquid to the desired consistency, but stir to prevent catching.

5 Serve with grated cheese on top.

Chicken chocolate molé

The word *molé* comes from an indigenous Mexican word meaning 'concoction' and applies to a variety of sauces there that are particularly good with chicken and turkey (and also with beef). One of the most famous variations includes a small amount of dark chocolate. This makes a delicious rich and creamy sauce, with interesting flavors, and goes well with pasta.

Some organic pasta is made in Italy from durum wheat and fairly traded flour from *quinoa*, a traditional cereal grown on the high slopes of the Andes in South America. The farmers who produce this are members of Anapqui, the umbrella organization of seven regional co-operatives. Most producers also cultivate potatoes and beans for their own families and keep llamas or sheep. Anapqui pays them a good price and this helps them to stay in their home area while others have to migrate in search of a better income.

Serves 2-3
Preparation: 15 minutes
Cooking: 55 minutes

INGREDIENTS

2 chicken breast fillets

1 tablespoon margarine

½ onion, chopped

1 clove garlic, minced

6 peppercorns

2 whole cloves

¼ cup / 60 ml tomato sauce

1 cup / 240 ml chicken stock/broth

½ slice bread

⅛ teaspoon anise seeds

1 teaspoon sugar

¼ teaspoon chili powder

1 tablespoon sesame seeds

¼ cup pignoles/pine nuts

3 wedges Mexican chocolate* or use 1 ounce / 25 g dark chocolate**

water

salt

* Such as Ibarra (small photo right), available from gourmetsleuth.com

** See note p 14

1 To begin, place the chicken breasts in a pan and pour in enough water to cover. Boil them for 20 minutes or so and then remove, retaining the stock/broth.

2 Now heat the margarine and cook the onion until it is soft. Add the garlic, peppercorns, cloves, tomato sauce, chicken stock, bread, anise, sugar, chili powder, sesame seeds and pignoles/pine nuts. Simmer gently for 20 minutes.

3 When ready, purée this sauce in a blender, adding more stock or water if required.

4 Then return the sauce to the pan on a low heat and add the chocolate, stirring to melt it.

5 Put in the chicken pieces and simmer gently for 10-15 minutes, stirring. Season, and serve with rice or pasta.

Chocolate and health

THERE HAVE ALWAYS been claims and counter-claims about the health-giving nature of chocolate. In the 17th century, physician Hans Sloane's cocoa was advertised as being 'greatly recommended by several eminent Physicians'. In the 1800s, doctors advised their lovelorn patients to eat chocolate to ease their broken hearts. In 1672, William Hughes wrote in *The American Physician*: 'Chocolate is most excellent, in nourishing and preserving health entire, preventing unnatural fumes ascending to the head.' Chocolate has been considered a remedy for a wide range of ills down the ages, from liver problems to consumption, fever and muscle diseases, hypochondria to hemorrhoids.

Cocoa cure: In the 19th century doctors prescribed 'flesh-forming' cocoa to plump up thin women. Note the Cadbury's advertisement on the doctor's surgery wall.

BETTMANN / CORBIS

- 1500s – A book written by a Mayan priest prescribed a bowl of chocolate containing two peppers, honey and tobacco juice as a remedy for skin eruptions, fever and seizures.
  - In 1552 the Badianus Manuscript had a remedy for injured feet involving a mixture of herbs and cacao flowers.
    - In 1592, Agustin Farfan's *Tratado Beve de Medicina* noted that chocolate can be used as a laxative.
    - 1741 – Linnaeus, who gave chocolate its botanical name, believed that chocolate could help wasting brought on by lung or muscle diseases, hypochondria and hemorrhoids.
    - 1846 – Anthelme Brillat-Savarin, a French lawyer, combined chocolate with ambergris (from whales) as a cure for hangovers, insomnia and problems of concentration.
- 1895-1930s – The major pharmaceutical companies all produced chocolate-covered pills to disguise the taste of their medicines. Rowntree in its early days offered 'Homeopathic chocolate'.
- 1983 – Dr Andrew Weil, author of *From Chocolate to Morphine*, said that chocolate was a drug: 'a mood-altering substance that can have strong effects on the body and mind and can certainly be addictive.'[4]

The cacao flower was used as a remedy for injured feet.

Eye on the prize: Chocoholics start young.

CORBIS

So IS CHOCOLATE really a drug, or an aphrodisiac, or even a health food? It is certainly complex, containing more than 300 chemical substances, including theobromine (affects the nervous system, increasing alertness and concentration) and anandamide (similar to the active ingredient in cannabis, which may explain any cravings). It also contains phenylethylamine (PEA), which is similar to the body's own adrenalin and dopamine (which as a drug is given to Parkinson's patients to stimulate the sympathetic nervous system) and can have mood-altering effects.

Turkey & bean chocolate chili

Just like some Mexican *molés* (sauces), this chili has a bit of chocolate in it. Serve yogurt or sour cream and grated cheddar cheese alongside. In Aztec times, Mexico's only domesticated animals were dogs and turkeys. According to Reay Tannahill's *Food in History*, the turkey was brought to Europe in the 16th century, probably traded by Levantine merchants – which is why it became known as 'turkey' in England. However in France it was called *dinde*, from *coq d'Inde*, ie from India. Meanwhile in India, the bird was called *peru*. And all probably because people could not get their tongues around the Aztec name, *uexolotl*.

Serves 6-8
Preparation: 10 minutes
Cooking: 35 minutes

INGREDIENTS

2 onions, chopped

2 red bell peppers, chopped

6 cloves garlic, chopped

2 pounds / 1 kg ground/ minced turkey

1-2 teaspoons chili powder

1½ teaspoons ground cumin

2 teaspoons dried oregano

2 cans pinto or red kidney beans, drained

2 cans tomatoes, with juice

3 cups chicken or vegetable stock

3 ounces / 75 g dark chocolate* chopped

oil

salt and pepper

* See note p 14

1 Heat the oil and then sauté the onions, bell peppers and garlic over a high heat until vegetables begin to soften, about 10 minutes.

2 Now add the turkey and fry for about 5 minutes, stirring, until it begins to brown.

3 At this point, mix in the chili powder, cumin and oregano and stir for a minute or so.

4 Then add the beans, tomatoes and juice, stock and chocolate. Season, and bring the chili to the boil.

5 Reduce heat and simmer uncovered until the mixture thickens, stirring occasionally, for about 20 minutes. Check the seasoning before serving.

Chicken-chocolate enchiladas

Chicken or turkey and chocolate go really well together, the chocolate giving a richness.
This Mexican-style dish can be made in advance and kept in the fridge.

Serves 6-8
Preparation: 30 minutes
Cooking: 1 hour

Ingredients

1 chicken, quartered

2½ cups / 590 ml chicken or vegetable broth/ stock

2 onions, finely chopped

4 cloves garlic, chopped

1 teaspoon dried oregano

1 teaspoon ground cumin

¼ teaspoon cinnamon

1 teaspoon chili powder

3 tablespoons flour

½ ounce / 15 g dark chocolate*

16 corn tortillas

1 pound / 450 g monterey jack or cheddar cheese, grated

1 cup pimiento-stuffed green olives, sliced

oil

salt and pepper

* See note p 14

Heat oven to 375°F/190°C/Gas 5

1 To begin, put the chicken and the stock in a large pot and bring to the boil. Then reduce the heat, partially cover the pan and simmer for 30 minutes or until the chicken is cooked. Leave the chicken to cool in the broth.

2 When ready, scoop off and discard any fat, and pour off the stock/broth (retain). Remove and discard the chicken skin and bones. Chop the chicken coarsely and then transfer it to large bowl.

3 Next, heat some oil in a saucepan and sauté the onions. When they are soft, add the garlic, oregano, cumin, cinnamon and chili powder; stir well and continue to cook for a few minutes.

4 Now mix in the flour and stir for a few seconds. Gradually whisk in half of the broth/stock. Bring to the boil and simmer for 15 minutes or until the liquid has thickened. Remove from the heat and add the chocolate; season with salt and pepper. Set aside.

5 Mix 1 cup of the sauce into the chicken. Arrange tortillas on a work surface and spoon 2 tablespoons of cheese, ½ tablespoon of olives, ½ tablespoon of sauce and a tablespoon of the chicken mix along the center of each, and then roll them up.

6 Arrange the enchiladas seam-side down in prepared dishes. Top the enchiladas with the sauce and sprinkle with cheese. Bake for 20 minutes. Serve them hot and bubbling, with salad.

Chili sin carne con chocolate*

Which means chili without meat but with chocolate... The taste of chocolate and chili is spreading: Italy's Cuba Venchi chocolate company even makes 'spiced up' bars, including ones with chili in them.

Serves 4
Preparation: 10 minutes
Cooking: 30 minutes

Heat oven to 350°F/180°C/Gas 4

INGREDIENTS

2 cans red kidney beans, drained (retain liquid)

2 onions, chopped

1 red bell pepper, sliced

3 cloves garlic, minced

1 teaspoon ground coriander

1 teaspoon ground cumin

1 teaspoon oregano

¼-½ teaspoon chili powder

1 cup / 110 g mushrooms, chopped

1 can tomatoes and juice

2 tablespoons tomato purée

¼ cup / 60 ml tarragon vinegar

3-4 ounces / 75-100 g dark chocolate*

oil

salt and pepper

* See note p 14

1 First fry the onions in oil in a large pan till golden. Then put in the red bell pepper, garlic, coriander, cumin, oregano and chili and fry gently. Put them into a deep ovenproof dish with a lid.

2 Add the beans, mushrooms, tomatoes and juice, tomato purée, vinegar and chocolate. Season; stir and pour in enough retained bean liquid or water just to cover.

3 Put the lid on the dish and bake for 20-30 minutes; if it seems to be drying out, add more liquid. This tastes even nicer when it is made the day before you want to eat it, and reheated.

*Vegan

Pure heaven

SCIENTISTS AT THE Massachusetts Institute of Technology (MIT) found that certain cells of the brain's hypothalamus send out pleasure signals in response to sweet or fatty substances. Chocolate is one of the few foods that are 50 per cent sugar and 50 per cent fat. 'That unique mixture of fat and sugar is pure heaven to our brains,' says nutrition researcher Michael Levine. 'Chemically speaking, chocolate really is the world's perfect food.'[5]

Inside chocolate

CHOCOLATE STARTS TO melt at body temperature – that's why it melts in your mouth. The nutritional content of chocolate varies according to the recipe. Generally, chocolate contains:

Protein – needed for cell maintenance and repair.
Fat – varies, but up to 50 per cent.
Vitamin E – a fat-soluble vitamin essential for cell membranes.
Calcium, phosphorus and **magnesium** – minerals essential for strong bones and teeth.
Iron – needed to form hemoglobin, the oxygen-carrying compound in blood.
Caffeine and **theobromine** – nervous system stimulants.
Copper – assists iron metabolism, formation of melanin (in hair and skin) and functioning of the central nervous system.
Sugar – varies, but often about 50 per cent.
Antioxidant phytochemicals (such as flavonoids) – cocoa beans, a main ingredient of chocolate (more so in dark chocolate), contain more than 600 plant chemicals, including antioxidants, that may protect against heart disease and cancer.[6]

Women & chocolate

WOMEN IN PARTICULAR are supposed to be chocolate lovers, perhaps because women are associated with sweet things. One of the largest studies in the US on food preferences found that 97 per cent of college women have specific food cravings – and they crave chocolate more than anything else. According to Italian researchers, women who regularly eat chocolate have a better sex life than those who don't. Urologists from San Raffaele hospital, Milan, questioned 163 women about their consumption of chocolate as well as their experience of sexual fulfillment. The study found: 'Women who have a daily intake of chocolate showed higher levels of desire than women who did not have this habit. Chocolate can have a positive physiological impact on a woman's sexuality.' Wishful thinking by male researchers? Dr Andrea Salonia, author of the study – funded from a university research budget, not by the confectionery industry – said women who have a low libido could even become more amorous after eating chocolate. 'Chocolate is not like a food, it is like a drug... I strongly believe eating chocolate may improve their sexual function,' he said.[7] No reports yet on what it does for men.

Chocoholics

PEOPLE HAVE LONG known that chocolate is not always good for you. Joseph Acosta, in 1604, described drinking chocolate as 'loathsome... having a skumme of froth that is very unpleasant to taste'. Chocolate has been blamed for acne, coronary heart disease, migraines, tooth decay and obesity.

It seems generally agreed that cocoa is better for you than chocolate – so eating dark chocolate or chocolate with a high cocoa content is preferable if you are a chocoholic. In Mexico, for example, dark chocolate is present in many of the savory *molés* (sauces), but combined with white meat and vegetables in this way gives it a lower energy density because it is being 'diluted' by the less energy-dense vegetables and meat.

• **MIGRAINES** Chocolate has been cited as a trigger for migraines. Research has shown that it is unlikely to cause migraines on its own, but combined with factors such as stress or hormonal imbalance, chocolate may also play a part.

French Kohler chocolate company poster, ca. 1938.

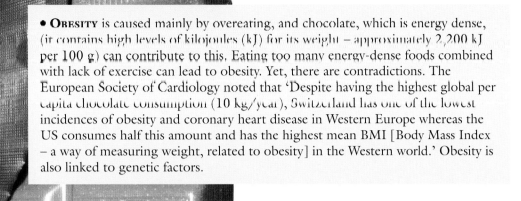

• **OBESITY** is caused mainly by overeating, and chocolate, which is energy dense, (it contains high levels of kilojoules (kJ) for its weight – approximately 2,200 kJ per 100 g) can contribute to this. Eating too many energy-dense foods combined with lack of exercise can lead to obesity. Yet, there are contradictions. The European Society of Cardiology noted that 'Despite having the highest global per capita chocolate consumption (10 kg/year), Switzerland has one of the lowest incidences of obesity and coronary heart disease in Western Europe whereas the US consumes half this amount and has the highest mean BMI [Body Mass Index – a way of measuring weight, related to obesity] in the Western world.' Obesity is also linked to genetic factors.

• **ACNE AND PIMPLES** The Better Health website notes that 'a recent Melbourne study has shown that around 70 per cent of people believe that certain foods can cause or exacerbate acne. Chocolate was indicated as one of the main culprits. There is no evidence to date to back up this long-held belief. However, some scientists now suggest that a high glycemic index* diet [foods that produce the highest blood sugar] combined with a high intake of refined carbohydrates (sugars, white flour etc), may be linked to pimples.'

* This is one way of categorizing foods by how rapidly they increase blood glucose levels, causing insulin to be released by the pancreas.

Danger: chocolate can kill your dog

THE DRUGS IN chocolate, theobromine and caffeine, are toxic to pets, and can be poisonous to dogs. Only a moderate amount needs to be eaten to be poisonous (approx. ½ ounce of baking chocolate per pound of body weight and less in some animals). Fortunately, the animal frequently vomits soon after.[8]

Pumpkin & chocolate chili

Delicious, and nice colors with the orange pumpkin, red bell pepper, green jalapeño, tomatoes and rich chocolate sauce.

Serves 4
Preparation: 20 minutes
Cooking: 30 minutes

INGREDIENTS

3 cups / 450 g cooked pumpkin

1 onion, chopped

1 red bell pepper, sliced

3 tablespoons jalapeño, sliced

1 clove garlic, minced

1 cup / 240 ml beer

1 cup / 240 ml stock

8 olives, sliced

1-2 teaspoons chili powder

1 teaspoon ground coriander

1 can tomatoes with juice

2 tablespoons cilantro/coriander, chopped

1 tablespoon cocoa

1-2 cans beans, such as pinto, white or kidney, drained

4-6 tablespoons scallions/spring onions, sliced

3 tablespoons cheddar cheese, grated

6 tablespoons sour cream or yogurt

oil

salt and pepper

1 Sauté the onion and when it is translucent, add the bell pepper, jalapeño and garlic; stir for 5 minutes.

2 Next, add the beer, stock, olives, chili powder, coriander and tomatoes with juice. Bring to the boil; reduce heat and simmer for 15 minutes.

3 The pumpkin goes in now, together with the cilantro/coriander, cocoa and beans. Stir well to combine the ingredients and season. Cook gently for 5 minutes or until the mix has cooked down and amalgamated.

4 Serve topped with the scallions/spring onion, cheese, and sour cream or yogurt.

Southwestern chili* with chocolate

Good rich flavor, nice and chocolatey. It can be made without the beef, but in that case use a whole can of beans and another bell pepper.

Serves 4
Preparation: 10 minutes
Cooking: 25 minutes

INGREDIENTS

1 pound / 450 g ground/ minced beef

2 onions, chopped

1 green bell pepper, chopped

3 cloves garlic, minced

1-2 teaspoons chili powder

1 tablespoon ground cumin

1 tablespoon dried oregano

1 can tomatoes, with juice

2 tablespoons tomato paste

½ can kidney beans, rinsed and drained

3 tablespoons cider vinegar

2 ounces / 50 g dark chocolate* chopped

oil

salt and pepper

For the toppings:

Tortilla chips

Sour cream or yogurt

Cheddar cheese, grated

1 red onion or 2 scallions/spring onion or a few chives, sliced finely

Jalapeño chili, sliced finely

* See note p 14

1 Start by sautéing the onions with the bell pepper in hot oil.

2 When the onion and pepper are soft, add the garlic and beef and stir to brown the beef all over.

3 Shake in the chili powder, cumin and oregano. Season, and stir as you cook for a further 2-3 minutes.

4 Now add the tomatoes and tomato paste, beans, vinegar, chocolate and mix round.

5 Simmer for about 15-20 minutes, stirring from time to time. Serve with the various toppings.

*Vegan adaptable

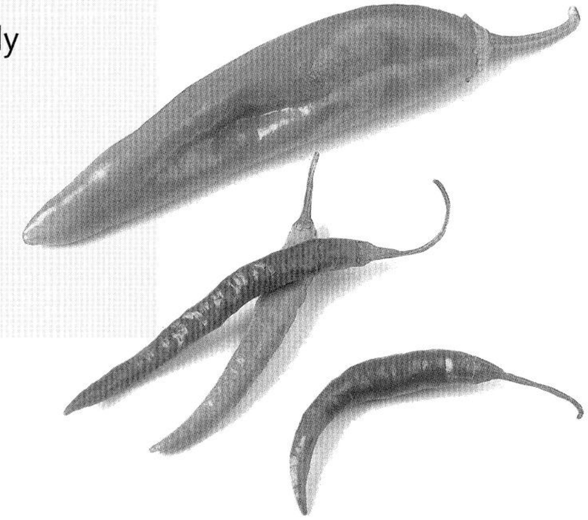

Chocolate around the world

WHATEVER THE DISPUTES around health, the fact remains that people in the rich world eat a lot of chocolate – 79 per cent of the total.
• The global confectionery market (including chocolate) reached an estimated value of $73.2 billion in 2001, a 21 per cent increase since 1996.
• The European market is the world's largest, accounting for 42 per cent of revenues for confectionery worldwide, followed by the Americas.
• 60 per cent of all chocolate is consumed in North America and the European Union (EU) – with only 20 per cent of the world population.[9]
• The US is the biggest importer of chocolate from Côte d'Ivoire, buying up about 70 per cent of the crop.[10]

As SEEN, THE Swiss top the chocolate league (see chart right). Since the start of the 1990s, Asia has developed into a major chocolate market. Japan has experienced a significant increase in chocolate consumption during the past decade. Demand in China increased to 9,000 tons in 2000, a rise of over 90 per cent from the previous year. Among cocoa-producing countries, Brazil has seen an increase of 10 per cent in its annual consumption per person since 1993.

Top chocoholics[11]

Country	Pounds	Kgs
	Average per year	
1 Switzerland	22.36	10.2
2 Austria	20.13	9.1
3 Ireland	19.47	8.9
4 Germany	18.04	8.2
5 Norway	17.93	8.1
6 Denmark	17.66	8.0
7 UK	17.49	7.9
8 Belgium	13.16	6.0
9 Australia	12.99	5.9
10 Sweden	12.90	5.9
11 United States	11.64	5.3
12 France	11.38	5.2
13 Netherlands	10.56	4.8
14 Finland	10.45	4.7
15 New Zealand	8.80	4.0
16 Canada	8.50	3.9
17 Italy	6.13	2.8
18 Greece	5.01	2.3
19 Japan	3.90	1.8
20 Spain	3.37	1.5
21 Portugal	2.67	1.2
22 Brazil	2.25	1.0

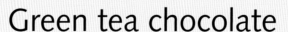

Green tea chocolate

MANY JAPANESE PEOPLE do not normally eat many sweet foods and prefer dark chocolate. Chocolate manufacturers are also promoting green tea chocolate, chocolate with sesame seeds or chocolate with small pieces of rice puff. Consumption of chocolate continues to grow, from 28,000 tons in 1960 to 110,000 tons in 1970 and 210,000 tons in 2004.

Cocoa for conservation

IN BAHIA, BRAZIL, cocoa is cultivated under thinned native trees in areas where little other forest remains. This helps conserve the existing forest. The majority of Brazil's cocoa is grown in this state, which has around 28,000 small cocoa farms – many owned by the farmers themselves. In 1989, 'witches broom' disease devastated the crop and output was halved over the following 10 years. Much of Brazil's cocoa is grown for domestic use.

Valentines in Japan

IN JAPAN, WOMEN are obliged to buy chocolate gifts for lovers, fathers, friends and male colleagues on St Valentine's Day. It was started by an entrepreneur in the late 1950s and reaps the country's chocolate industry nearly 20 per cent of its annual 400 billion yen in sales.

There are two kinds of chocolate gifts on this day: *giri choco* (obligatory chocolate) and *honmei choco* (chocolate for the man the woman is serious about). *Giri choco* is given by women to their superiors at work as well as to other male co-workers. It is not unusual for a woman to

buy 20 to 30 boxes of this type of chocolate for distribution at home and at work.

The tradition is said to have begun in February 1958 when Kunio Hara, president of Mary's chocolate company, hit upon the idea of selling chocolates as Valentine's Day gifts. Mary's sales increased by some 30 per cent from 1958 to 1960. Other manufacturers soon followed suit. And so that men did not feel left out, in 1980 confectioners created 'White Day' when men are obliged to buy chocolates in white boxes for the women in their lives.[12]

China's sweet tooth

AS CHINA'S ECONOMY expands, so does its taste for luxuries, with people eating over two pounds of confectionery each per year. China's candy market is worth $4.3 billion. But sales of chocolate are set to triple between 1998 and 2008. And foreign companies are keen to be the first to exploit the country's increasingly sweet tooth. Even if only two per cent of the population can afford luxury chocolate, this is still 30 million people. At China's first candy fair in November 2004,

JACOB LOTINGA

70 per cent of the exhibitors were foreign companies. Jeff de Bruges, a French luxury chocolate retailer, recently opened its first shop in Shanghai with a local partner. The manager, Philippe Jamba, said it was a test venture in a market that is still more about potential than current sales. 'We have to tell people what chocolate is about. It is a huge education process.'[13]

Vegan chocolate cake

This is simple and quick to make. It is moist, light and quite crumbly. While chocolate is sweet for us, it can be heartbreaking for cocoa producers and their families. In 2001, The US State Department and the ILO reported child slavery on Côte d'Ivoire cocoa farms, the origin of 43 per cent of the world's cocoa. The solution is fair trade which ensures that producers earn enough to send their kids to school and pay their workers. See campaigning organizations on p 170.

Preparation: 10 minutes
Cooking: 40 minutes

Heat oven to 350°F/180°C/Gas 4

INGREDIENTS

1½ cups / 185 g flour

¾ cup / 130 g brown sugar

1 teaspoon baking soda

½ teaspoon salt

3 tablespoons cocoa powder

1 tablespoon vinegar

⅓ cup / 75 ml oil

1 teaspoon vanilla

¼ teaspoon cinnamon

1 cup / 240 ml water

1 In a large bowl, mix all the ingredients together and stir well.

2 Grease and line a cake tin or small loaf tin and then pour in the mixture.

3 Bake for 30-40 minutes or until skewer comes out clearly. When ready, turn out of the tin and cool on a rack.

Brazil nut cake with chocolate chips

CAI Campesino in Bolivia supplies Brazil nuts. It is a co-operative, which sells on behalf of over 300 nut-gathering families, widely scattered in the Amazon forest.

Preparation: 20 minutes
Cooking: 1½ hours

INGREDIENTS

1 cup / 100 g dates, chopped

1 cup / 100 g Brazil nuts, chopped

¼ cup / 25 g glacé cherries, halved

1 cup / 100 g chocolate chips*

¾ cup / 100 g flour

½ teaspoon baking powder

pinch salt

¾ cup / 130 g brown sugar

3 eggs, separated

* See note p 14

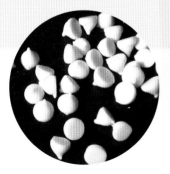

Heat oven to 375°F/190°C/Gas 5

1 Put the chopped dates and nuts into a bowl and then add the cherries and chocolate chips.

2 Next, sift the flour, baking powder and salt into the bowl, together with the sugar. Stir well.

3 Whisk the egg whites until frothy. Stir the yolks into the whites and then add this mixture to the bowl.

4 Stir well to integrate the ingredients and then spoon into a greased 2-pound/1-kg loaf tin and bake for 1½ hours or so. Leave to cool in the tin for 15 minutes and then turn out onto a wire rack.

The sticky world of Big Chocolate

'MOVING TO HERSHEY was like moving to paradise; no more outhouses or one-room schoolhouses or dirt roads. We had steam heat and electricity and telephones. And the streets were cobblestone. That was something.'[14]

MONROE STOVER, ONE OF THE EARLY WORKERS AT HERSHEY.

Marble chocolate cake

It's always fascinating to see the way the two colors of the cake align themselves, separate but intertwined.

Preparation: 20 minutes
Cooking: 40 minutes

INGREDIENTS

1 cup / 225 g margarine or butter

1 cup / 225 g sugar

½ teaspoon vanilla

3 eggs, beaten

2½ cups / 300 g flour, sifted

1 teaspoon baking powder

3 ounces / 75 g chocolate*

* See note p 14

Heat oven to 350°F/180°C/Gas 4

1 Start by creaming the margarine or butter with the sugar to make fluffy mixture; add the vanilla.

2 Gradually add the beaten eggs, alternating with flour to make a smooth mixture.

3 Divide the mixture and put half into another bowl. Melt the chocolate in a basin over a pan of boiling water and beat this into one of the bowls of cake mix.

4 Place alternate small spoonfuls of plain and chocolate mixture into the cake tin and then bake for 40 minutes or so. Leave to cool in the tin for a few minutes and then turn out onto a rack to finish cooling.

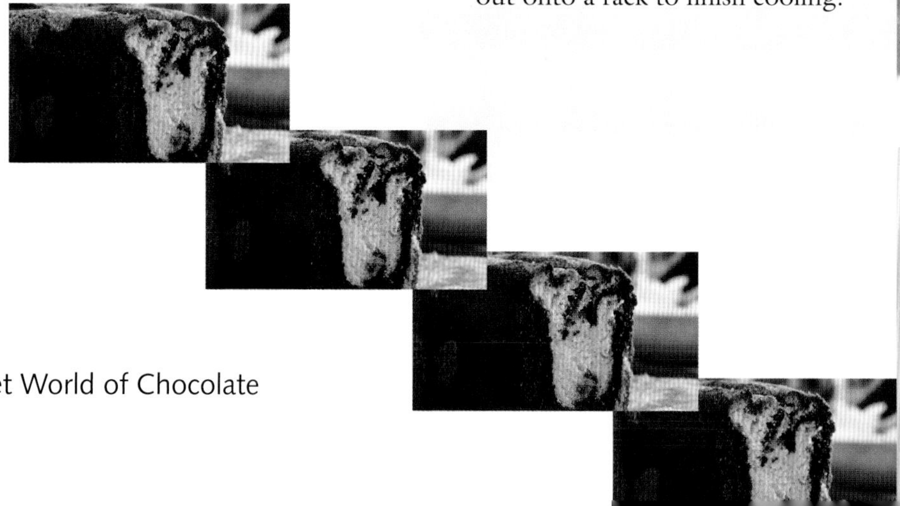

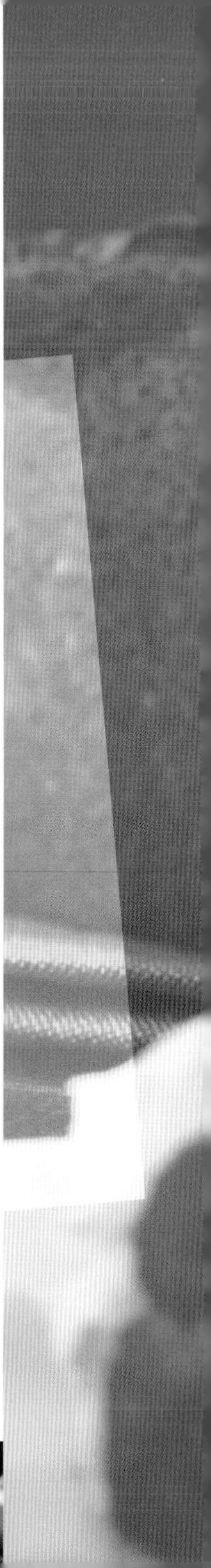

Chocolate banana bread

By 2002, fair-trade bananas were being exported from small farmers' associations or co-operatives and plantations in Ghana, Ecuador, the Dominican Republic, Colombia, Costa Rica, St Lucia, St Vincent, Dominica and Grenada. All three organizations in the Dominican Republic and one in Ecuador produce certified organic bananas. However, trade policy changes threaten fair-trade farmers in the Windward Islands.

Preparation: 20 minutes
Cooking: 1 hour

INGREDIENTS

4 ripe bananas, mashed

1¾ cups / 225 g flour

3 tablespoons cocoa

2 teaspoons baking powder

1 cup / 175 g brown sugar

4 eggs, beaten

1 teaspoon vanilla

½ teaspoon cinnamon

pinch of salt

½ cup / 50 g raisins or sultanas

3 tablespoons chopped walnuts +

+ optional

Heat oven to 350°F/180°C/Gas 4

1 Start by sifting the flour, cocoa, baking powder and salt into a bowl, and then add the sugar.
2 In a separate bowl, combine the bananas, eggs, vanilla and cinnamon. Now add them to the dry ingredients, plus the raisins or sultanas and nuts if using, and stir to combine.
3 Grease an 8-inch/20-cm loaf tin and then pour in the mix.
4 Bake for about an hour and when it is ready, remove from the oven and leave to cool for 15 minutes in the tin. Then turn out onto a rack. When cool, dust with icing sugar or cocoa.

Quakers saw chocolate as a benign substitute for alcohol.

STRANGE AS IT may seem, a number of the really big names in chocolate today had their roots in religion. In Britain, Cadburys, Fry's, Rowntree's and Terry's were all founded with money from Quaker families. In the US, Milton Hershey (1857-1945), who started the Hershey chocolate company, was of Mennonite stock.[15] Part of the inspiration, particularly for the Quakers, came from the fact that chocolate was seen as a benign substitute for alcohol – the one a sin, the other merely a minor vice. The founders built towns for their workers and provided housing, schools, churches and parks for their spiritual as well as their material well-being.

The town of Hershey, built in 1903, provided workers' housing that was way ahead of most such accommodation in big cities.

Hershey's model town

THE TOWN OF Hershey, built in 1903, had Chocolate and Cocoa Avenues and streetlights shaped like Hershey's Kisses chocolates. At its heart was the factory, designed to accommodate 600 workers and produce millions of dollars' worth of chocolate each year. At a time when workers in London or New York were living in the most squalid of slums, Hershey's employees' houses were each individually designed with plumbing and electricity. The town was full of greenery, with an enormous park in the center. There were five golf courses, a zoo, a post office, and five churches. The Pennsylvania legislature hailed it as a 'model town'. By 1909 it included an inn, a restaurant, a gym and a swimming pool. By 1913 the total population was 700 but there were more than 100,000 visitors a year. Alongside the town, Hershey built an orphanage and in 1918 set up a Trust to ensure that it would always have funding. William Dearden, who became Chief Executive at Hershey in 1965, had once been a boy from the Hershey orphanage.

NAJLAH FEANNY/CORBIS

Chocolate and war

Joel Glenn Brenner's book *The Emperors of Chocolate* starts with a battle during the first Gulf War in 1991. A battle not, as you might think, between the Iraqis and the Allied Forces, but between Mars and Hershey. Their ultimate goal? The contract for the supply of non-melting chocolate bars to US, British and Saudi soldiers, worth around $1.2 million. The engagement was bitter, the battle fast and furious. Paul Lieberman, attorney for the US General Accounting Office, was amazed: 'The way Hershey was complaining, you'd have thought that Mars was breaching national security by selling military secrets or something. But... this contract was for chocolate for goodness' sake.'

In fact Mars and Hershey were building on a long and lucrative link between chocolate and the military. Four centuries earlier, Aztec warriors were given the drink to boost morale; in the 19th century the Royal Navy consumed more than half the cocoa imported into Britain. In 1823, British seamen were given a ration of an ounce of cocoa a day – it was considered the ideal drink as it was hot, healthy and non-alcoholic.

In the First World War, American soldiers were supplied with chocolate by Hershey, who produced 'Field Ration D', a 600-calorie bar made from chocolate liquor, sugar, oat flour, powdered milk and vitamins that could withstand temperatures up to 120° Fahrenheit (50° Celsius). A poster for an American aid organization in 1914 asked people to: 'Send 'em a smoke, send 'em a sweet. Your boy needs tobacco, chocolate, jam.' Robert Whymper, who worked for the British chocolate industry, wrote in 1921 that: 'Without tobacco, rum and chocolate... an army in warfare would be defeated even with a sufficiency of guns and ammunition.' More than three billion Ration Ds were churned out during the Second World War. In 1942 the Quartermaster-General came to Hershey to present it with the military's highest award for civilian contributions to victory.

Irish potato cake with chocolate

Two New World ingredients meet up in a intriguing combination...
and it is a nice cake.

Preparation: 15 minutes
Cooking: 40 minutes

Heat oven to 350°F/180°C/Gas 4

INGREDIENTS

½ cup / 110 g margarine or butter

1 cup / 175 g brown sugar

2 eggs, beaten

1 cup / 110 g cold mashed potato

2 teaspoons cocoa

½ teaspoon cinnamon

¼ teaspoon nutmeg

1 cup / 125 g flour

1 teaspoon baking soda

½ cup / 110 ml yogurt or sour milk

½ cup / 50 g nuts, coarsely chopped

1 Begin by creaming the margarine or butter with the sugar to make a light mixture.

2 Now add the beaten eggs and mix well before putting in the mashed potato, cocoa, cinnamon and nutmeg.

3 When ready, sift the flour with the baking soda and add to the chocolate mixture alternately with the yogurt or sour milk. Mix well.

4 Now add the nuts and stir them in.

5 Spoon the mixture into an 8-inch/20-cm greased baking pan and cook for 30-40 minutes, or until a skewer comes out cleanly. Cool in the pan before serving.

Chocolate carrot cake*

Another vegan cake. Try using fairly traded Demerara sugar from Mauritius; some of these sugars are packed on the island by an organization providing work for disabled people.

Preparation: 15 minutes
Cooking: 30 minutes

Heat oven to 350°F/180°C/Gas 4

INGREDIENTS

1 cup / 100 g grated carrots

1 cup / 175 g brown sugar

½ cup / 120 ml oil

1 cup / 240 ml boiling water

1¼ cups / 150 g wholewheat flour

½ cup / 60 g cocoa

1 teaspoon cinnamon

1½ teaspoons baking powder

pinch of salt

1 Using a large bowl, mix the carrot with the sugar and oil and then pour the boiling water over the mixture. Stir, and then set aside

2 Next, combine the flour, cocoa, cinnamon, baking powder and salt in a separate bowl. Sift this into the carrot mixture and stir well.

3 Grease an 8-inch/20-cm tin and bake for 30 minutes or so. Leave in the tin for 10 minutes and then turn out onto a rack to cool.

*Vegan

Cadbury's Bournville

IN BRITAIN IN the 1870s, George and Richard Cadbury had set up Bournville for their workers. George was a housing reformer: living conditions for most people in Britain at the time were appalling. A Royal Commissioners' report in the 1840s showed that a quarter of Birmingham's population of 220,000 lived in undrained streets, many of which were quagmires. The death rate there was twice that of Edgbaston, a suburb a few miles from the city center.[16]

The Cadburys, a Quaker family, had founded their chocolate business back in 1831, when John Cadbury first made cocoa products on a factory scale in an old malthouse in Birmingham. When their factory became too small, the brothers had an idea: 'Why should an industrial area be squalid and depressing? Why should not the industrial worker enjoy country air and occupations without being separated from his

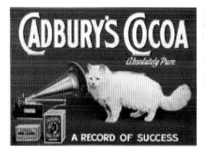

(Left and below) Cadbury's was founded in 1831. Bournville in Birmingham, UK, housed their workers, and was part of the 'Garden City' movement.

work? If the country is a good place to live in, why not to work in?'

By 1900, the estate included 330 acres of land with 313 cottages. Cadbury then set up a Trust. Unlike Hershey, the town was not only for the benefit of Cadbury workers but for others as well. It was also separate from the Cadbury Company. It became part of the burgeoning Garden City Movement that was very popular at the time. By 1915, the general death rate and infant mortality in Bournville was significantly lower than in the rest of Birmingham.

Joseph Rowntree, another Quaker, had similar principles to the Cadburys. Under the Joseph Rowntree Village Trust, he set up the model village of New Earswick for people on low incomes. The Village Trust eventually became the Joseph Rowntree Foundation which today supports an annual £7/$12 million program of research and development in the fields of housing, social care and social policy in the UK.

WHERE BOURNVILLE · COCOA IS MADE

Today's giants

THE MAJOR CHOCOLATE companies have become huge multinational corporations, accountable only to shareholders, whose main priority is the bottom line and who play a cut-throat game of takeovers and profits. In the last 10 years the price of cocoa beans has halved, but the price of a bar of chocolate has increased by two-thirds. And it is clear that it is not the small cocoa farmers who are making all the money.

The Big Five

TODAY, A FEW giant corporations control the chocolate market. Mars and Hershey's eat up three-quarters of US chocolate sales, while Cadbury, Nestlé and Mars devour the same proportion in Britain. These companies, with Ferrero, dominate retail sales of chocolate.[17] In 2003, the total sales of the top 10 chocolate companies amounted to $41,921 million. The net annual sales of Mars are higher than the gross national product of 81 countries.

Top 10

THE TOP 10 global confectionery companies that manufacture some form of chocolate, by total confectionery sales value:[18]

Company	Total sales $ millions
Mars Inc (US)	8,145
Nestlé SA (Switzerland)	7,771
Cadbury Schweppes PLC (UK)	5,890
Ferrero SpA (Italy)	4,769
Hershey Foods Corp. (US)	4,120
Kraft Foods (US)	3,122
Wm.Wrigley Jr. Co. (US)	2,746
Barry Callebaut AG (Switzerland)	2,547
Perfetti Van Melle SpA (Italy)	1,599
Lindt & Sprungli (Switzerland)	1,212
Total	**41,921**

The BitterSweet World of Chocolate

Chocolate cake with lemon filling

Moist and rich, and the lemony filling gives a nice boost. Molasses or black treacle, used here, is a thick, syrupy derivative of sugar cane. The quality of molasses depends on the maturity of the cane, the amount of sugar extracted, and the method of extraction. It is a good source of iron and essential B vitamins.

Preparation: 20 minutes
Cooking: 25 minutes

Heat oven to 350°F/180°C/Gas 4

INGREDIENTS

¾ cup / 110 g flour

1 teaspoon baking powder

¼ teaspoon baking soda

pinch salt

1 ounce / 25 g chocolate*

½ cup / 120 ml milk

⅓ cup / 75 g margarine or butter

¾ cup / 130 g brown sugar

2 eggs

½ tablespoon molasses/black treacle

½ teaspoon vanilla

FOR FILLING:

½ cup / 75 g margarine or butter

2 tablespoons icing sugar

1 tablespoon cocoa

juice of ½ -1 lemon

* See note p 14

1 Start by mixing together the flour, baking powder and soda plus the salt in a bowl.

2 Place the chocolate with the milk into a pan and heat very gently, stirring to melt the chocolate; then set aside to cool.

3 In a bowl, cream the margarine or butter and sugar together until light and fluffy.

4 Now beat in the eggs, one by one, sifting in a little of the flour mixture with each one.

5 Stir in the molasses/treacle and vanilla, and add the remaining flour. Mix well.

6 Next, spoon the cooled chocolate into the flour mixture and stir to create a batter.

7 Divide the mixture between 2 greased tins and then bake for 25 minutes or so, until springy to the touch. Cool the cakes on a rack.

8 For the filling, cream the margarine or butter with the icing sugar and cocoa, and add lemon juice to taste. Adjust the consistency by adding more dry ingredients or juice as required. Spread it on one of the cooled cakes and then sandwich the cake together. Dust the top with icing sugar.

Oat & chocolate cupcakes

Great cupcakes with very little fat, especially if you use skimmed milk. For those who appreciate the pure taste of good cocoa, fairly traded varieties offer yet another way to indulge in chocolate and ensure a fair deal for small-scale cocoa farmers.

Makes 12-16
Preparation: 10 minutes
Cooking: 25 minutes

Heat oven to 350°F/180°C/Gas 4

INGREDIENTS

1 cup / 125 g flour

½ cup / 50 g oats

½ cup / 60 g cocoa

1½ teaspoons baking powder

1½ teaspoons baking soda

½ teaspoon salt

1 egg

1 tablespoon oil

1 teaspoon vanilla

½ teaspoon cinnamon

1 cup / 175 g brown sugar

¼ cup / 60 ml milk

1 Combine the flour with the oats, cocoa, baking powder, baking soda and salt.

2 In a large bowl, beat together the egg, oil, vanilla, cinnamon and sugar.

3 Now stir in the flour mixture, gradually adding the milk until just combined. Pour the batter into paper cake cups.

4 Bake for 20-25 minutes or until a skewer comes out clean. Let the cupcakes cool on a wire rack.

Chocolate and advertising

Is consumption of chocolate linked to the many adverts for chocolate products? Companies spend large percentages of their budget on advertising their products; for example, in 2002, the Nestlé company spent £6.5 million ($11.7 million) on advertising its Kit-Kat bar. Marion Nestlé (no relation), nutritionist and former editor of the US Surgeon-General's report on Nutrition and Health, notes: 'To satisfy stockholders, food companies must convince people to eat more of their products instead of those of their competitors. They do so through advertising and public relations, of course, but also by working tirelessly to convince government officials, nutrition professionals and also the media that their products promote health – or at least do no harm.'[19]

(Below and opposite page) Classic Suchard advertisements, ca. 1901-33, combine racism, adventure and chocolate in a heady mix.

Cocoa's colonial past

CHOCOLATE ADVERTISEMENTS DATE back to the 19th century and reflect the colonial past. A set of Suchard posters from the early 20th century sees the bringing of chocolate as a true colonial adventure. They feature chocolate's journey across continents. It starts in America – a white man in cowboy hat on a white horse is accompanied by Native Americans, a bar of chocolate in the background. Then he is on a mule, with a bevy of black servants carrying his luggage, all presumably rushing to bring chocolate to the hungry hordes back home. The pyramids can be seen in the background. The third features the same person, this time lounging in a canoe as he is paddled by people who are presumably Africans, though clad in feathers and armed with arrows. And finally, in a fourth poster, he has arrived in Britain, triumphantly bearing his chocolate in a horse and cart, surrounded by a band playing bagpipes and a Guardsman in red and black, the Houses of Parliament in the background. No black people in sight this time.

CHOCOLAT SUCHARD

LEONARD DE SELVA / CORBIS

CHOCOLAT SUCHARD

EVEN IN THOSE days, advertisements told people that chocolate would improve their lives, their health and that of their children – and delight their taste buds. Sex simmers subtly in the background. A poster of a man and a woman, smartly dressed, sharing a box of Mackintosh's Quality Street was accompanied by this adage: 'A seat in the sun, the scent of flowers... and everything in the garden is lovely! Lovelier still if you have Quality Street....' In other words, it only takes Quality Street, love and sunshine to make life perfect. There is also a hint of the psychological comfort that chocolate is supposed to provide. A 2002 Hershey's advertisement pointed out that though your girlfriend may leave you, chocolate never will. Similarly, Cadbury's made a quirky series of advertisements in the 1970s

explaining that although the world is modernizing, with everything from high-rise apartments to jet planes, you still have Cadbury's Dairy Milk. This sense of chocolate as security seems to be borne out in reality as well. Claes Fornell, director of the American Customer Satisfaction Index (ACSI), noted that 'the public's concern about safety, the war in Iraq, rising healthcare costs and oil prices, all fueled by the presidential election campaign, may have contributed to rising customer satisfaction with chocolate, candy, and cigarettes.'[20]

Today, advertising is increasing in countries which are not traditional consumers of chocolate – one survey in India showed that chocolate advertising on television had increased by 23 per cent in the first half of 2004 compared to the same period of 2003.

Vegan chocolate sponge cake

Fine and light. Honey can be used for the filling – try fair-trade honey from Zambia or Chile:

'Apicoop [honey supplier] gives us a permanent market for our products and this helps us develop. Before we kept bees we had no jobs and now we have been able to develop ourselves as people and the bees have become a social thing as they are helping the community grow and develop in a harmonious way,' say Sonia and Celia, who manage about 30 hives as business partners in Calcurrupes, Chile.

Preparation: 15 minutes
Cooking: 40 minutes

Heat oven to 325°F/160°C/Gas 3

INGREDIENTS

2 cups / 225 g self-rising flour

¼ cup / 30 g cocoa

3 teaspoons baking powder

¾ cup / 150 g sugar

9 tablespoons oil

1½ cups / 350 ml water

1 Sift the flour, cocoa and baking powder into a bowl. Add the sugar, oil and water.

2 Next, mix well to a batter-like consistency. Grease two shallow cake pans and line with a circle of greased wax paper.

3 Pour the mixture into the prepared pans and bake for about 40 minutes, until the cakes are springy to the touch.

4 Turn the cakes out on to a wire rack and leave to cool.

5 Sandwich together with jam or honey and sift a little icing sugar as topping, if liked.

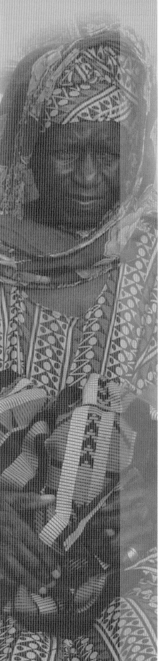

Fruitcake with chocolate

Sher Ghazi, the Administator, talks about the Dried Fruit Project in the Karakorum Mountains of Pakistan: 'The people in the northern hills produce a healthy fruit. Although we are not certified organically, I am sure nobody has ever used any chemical on the apricot trees. So I am sure this is a healthy fruit that has zero value in the local market, but it has a high nutritional value and people will understand the quality. I hope the people will enjoy eating the fruit and also be satisfied buying it, because the money goes to the poorest of the poor.'

Preparation: 10 minutes
Cooking: 40 minutes

Heat oven to 350°F/180°C/Gas 4

INGREDIENTS

1 cup / 225 g margarine

1 ounce / 25 g semisweet chocolate

1 cup / 175 g brown sugar

4 eggs

1 cup / 125 g flour

1 teaspoon baking powder

pinch of salt

1 cup / 100 g sultanas or raisins

1 cup / 100 g other dried fruit, such as dates or apricots, chopped

¾ cup / 100 g walnut halves

¾ cup / 100 g pecan halves or other nuts

1 First, using a heavy pan, melt the margarine and chocolate over a low heat, stirring frequently. Then remove from the heat and leave to cool for 10 minutes or so.

2 Then add the sugar and add the eggs, one by one, stirring well after each one.

3 The flour, baking powder and salt can be sifted in now; stir until the ingredients are blended.

4 Finally, put in the fruit and nuts and stir again.

5 Grease and flour a small loaf tin and then spoon in the mixture.

6 Bake for 35-40 minutes or until a skewer comes out clean. Cool the cake in the tin for 10 minutes and then turn out onto a rack.

The source of
our delight

'ONCE WE WERE warriors and triumphed over our enemies. Now we are farmers and fight the bush.'[21]

KOTO ASAMOAH SEREBOUR, COCOA FARMER, GHANA.

Chocolate raspberry shortcakes

The small-scale growers of the CONACADO co-operative in the Dominican Republic carefully cultivate their cocoa trees with gentle, shade-grown, chemical-free farming methods. This creates the natural environment preferred by cocoa trees as well as native wildlife and migratory birds. Then the co-op selects the best beans for special post-harvest processing, including a critical three-day fermentation stage. Finally, in Holland, the cocoa nibs are processed to create premier cocoa.

Makes 6-8
Preparation: 10 minutes
Cooking: 10 minutes

INGREDIENTS

½ cup / 60 g flour

2 tablespoons cocoa

2 tablespoons sugar

¼ teaspoon baking powder

¼ teaspoon baking soda

pinch salt

a little milk

2 tablespoons margarine or butter

FOR THE TOPPING:

1 cup / 100 g raspberries

1 tablespoon sugar, or to taste

¼ cup / 60 ml whipping cream

Heat oven to 425°F/220°C/Gas 7

1 In a bowl, mix together the flour, cocoa, sugar, baking powder, baking soda, and salt.

2 Then cut in the margarine or butter and blend the mixture until it looks like breadcrumbs.

3 Add enough milk to make a stiff dough.

4 Roll out the dough to a thickness of ½ inch/ 1 cm on a floured surface. Cut into shapes with a cookie cutter.

5 Grease a baking tray and then bake for 5-10 minutes until cooked. Leave to cool for a few minutes before placing onto a rack to cool.

6 In a bowl, mash the raspberries with a fork and add a little sugar if desired.

7 Whip the cream until it is stiff and then add the raspberry mixture, combining well. Spoon some onto each shortbread, and serve.

Oatmeal chocolate cake

Oats are good for you, although chocolate may be less so – however there are studies linking cocoa with health benefits. The darker chocolate with the most concentrated cocoa is the most beneficial. No doubt over-indulgence and the sugar load are the real problems for chocoholics.

Preparation: 10 minutes
Cooking: 35 minutes

Heat oven to 350°F/180°C/Gas 4

INGREDIENTS

½ cup / 50 g oats

1 teaspoon baking soda

½ cup / 120 ml boiling water

½ cup / 110 g margarine or butter

1 cup / 175 g brown sugar

2 eggs

1 teaspoon vanilla

1 cup / 125 g flour

1 teaspoon baking powder

4 tablespoons cocoa

pinch salt

1 Put the oats and baking soda into a small bowl and pour the boiling water over; stir and set aside.

2 Using a large bowl, cream the margarine or butter with the sugar. Then beat in the eggs, one at a time and add the vanilla.

3 In a separate bowl, mix the flour with the baking powder, cocoa and salt.

4 Now, add alternately some of the oats mixture and some of the flour mixture to the bowl of eggs and sugar, stirring to mix well.

5 Pour the cake mix into a greased tin and bake for 30-35 minutes.

The source of our delight

THAT SWEET TASTE on your tongue can be traced back to *theobroma cacao*, the tree of the gods, which probably originated thousands of years ago in the rainforests of South America. In the wild, the cocoa tree can grow up to 10 or 15 meters, and lives protected by other taller trees. At least 80 per cent of the foods used by the developed world come from the rainforest including avocados, bananas, cocoa, coconuts, mangoes, maize/corn, pineapples, potatoes, rice, tomatoes, squash, yams and many spices.

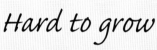

Hard to grow

A COCOA TREE NEEDS:
80 inches of rain
Shade
High humidity
At least 65° Fahrenheit
(18° Celsius)

DAY CHOCOLATE

Opening cocoa pods, Kuforidua, Ghana. During the main harvest (October-December) a farmer may cut down 3,000 cocoa pods a day from the trees.

THE CACAO PODS are oval-shaped and grow directly out of the trunk and branches rather than at the ends of the branches like other fruit. There are several different species of the tree, which grow in countries between about 20° north and 20° south of the Equator.

• The original one is called *Criollo* (Spanish for native-born) and is still grown in South America and also in Indonesia. It is used to make high-quality chocolate but is not very hardy or fruitful and accounts for about five per cent of the world's cocoa.

• *Forastero* (foreign) is in fact a native of the Amazon and has become the most popular variety, also grown all over Africa and Asia because it produces a lot of pods. It is the most common type of cocoa tree.

• *Trinitario* is a hybrid of the first two and was originally developed in Trinidad. It is now grown in all cocoa-producing areas, and makes up between 10 and 15 per cent of the cocoa in the world.

Cocoa tree facts

- The blossoms are pollinated by midges.
- The pods do not naturally fall to the forest floor. They are carried by monkeys, bats and other animals who chew through the outside and release the bitter seeds.
- It takes five years for a tree to produce its first crop and six months for a pod to ripen.
- A good tree will produce about 50 pods twice a year.
- The pods grow to about 8 inches long and 4 inches wide and turn red, yellow or orange when they are ripe.
- Inside are 40 almond-sized seeds in a sweet, creamy-colored pulp – enough to make four bars of dark chocolate or twice that amount of milk chocolate.
- The tree bears fruit for about 30 years.

Asamoah Serebour and his wife Kate on their farm near Sankari, Ghana.

SARAH ERRINGTON / HUTCH NCSN

A 1900 book described the ideal spot to start a plantation as 'a well-sheltered vale, covered with large trees, protected by mountain spur from the prevailing winds, well watered, and yet well drained, with a good depth of alluvial soil, on which rests a thick deposit of decayed vegetable matter, easy of access, and in a district distant from lagoons or marshes, for the sake of the proprietor's health.'[22] It has not been easy for cacao growers to replicate the rainforest. But by far the most serious problem has been pests and diseases such as plant rot and fungus. Even under the best circumstances, 30 per cent of the crop is lost in this way.

Pesticides

ONE OF THE obvious ways to reduce pests is to use pesticides. And in many cocoa-producing countries, pesticides are not controlled. Lindane, a hormone disrupter linked to breast cancer, was banned in Europe in 1991. A UK Friends of the Earth survey tested cooking chocolate in 1997 and found that all samples contained pesticides, including inorganic bromide and lindane.[23] Continental chocolate was tested in 1998: 12 out of 16 samples contained the same pesticide. In 1998, the *Annual Report of the Pesticide Residues Committee* found that 11 of 15 samples of continental chocolate contained detectable residues. An Austrian report in 1998 concluded that it is not possible to set a safe exposure level for lindane.

In Ghana, lindane has been widely used on cocoa crops. In December 1996, Ghana's Parliament passed the Pesticides Control and Management Act. The law empowers the Ghana Environmental Protection Agency (EPA) to regulate production, importation, distribution, handling and use of pesticides. It also grants Ghana EPA the power to enforce pesticide laws.

Barbara Dinham of the Pesticides Action Network UK says: 'Retailers and consumers have a responsibility to support cleaner and safer ways of producing chocolate. Cocoa farmers are interested in growing organic cocoa but need government, industry and consumer support to do so. Ghanaian environmentalists are extremely concerned that cocoa pesticides including lindane are also being used on local crops, with serious risks to human health.'[24]

Cocoa products

MANY DIFFERENT SORTS of products can be derived from cocoa. The husks of cocoa pods and the pulp, or 'sweatings', surrounding the beans and the cocoa bean shells can be used. Some examples of these uses are:

• **Animal feed from husks** – The animal feed is produced by first slicing the fresh cocoa husks into small flakes and then partially drying the flakes, followed by mincing and drying of the pellets.
• **Production of soft drinks and alcohol** – In the preparation of soft drinks, fresh cocoa pulp juice (sweatings) is collected, sterilized and bottled. For the production of alcoholic drinks, such as brandy, the fresh juice is boiled, cooled and fermented with yeast.

After four days' fermentation, the alcohol is distilled.
• **Potash from cocoa pod husks** – Cocoa pod husk ash is used mainly for soft soap manufacture. It may also be used as fertilizer for cocoa, vegetables, and food crops. To prepare the ash, fresh husks are spread out in the open to dry for one to two weeks. The dried husks are then incinerated in an ashing kiln.
• **Jam and marmalade** – Pectin for jam and marmalade is extracted from the sweatings by precipitation with alcohol, followed by distillation and recycling of the alcohol in further extractions.
• **Mulch** – Cocoa bean shells can be used as an organic mulch and soil conditioner for the garden.

Bringing back the cocoa pods, Ghana.

BRIAN MOODY / DAY CHOCOLATE

Philip with cocoa pod, Ghana.

From cocoa to chocolate

HARVESTING COCOA IS hard work. The trees take five years to mature. Plantations may be a long way from home, and the pods have to be cut from the trees by hand with machetes. A day or two later, the pods are split and the beans inside removed by hand along with the slippery pulp. Exposed to the air, the beans start to turn darker, but still do not smell or look like chocolate.

The next stage is fermentation. The beans and pulp are put in sacks in large wooden boxes, sometimes covered with banana leaves, and allowed to 'sweat' for four to seven days. During the process, yeasts and bacteria fed by the pulp increase the temperature of the beans and this causes a chemical change: the sugars are converted to lactic and acetic acid. The heat also produces enzymes which, when heated, will reduce the bitter flavor of the bean.

The beans are then spread out to dry in the sun for about a week. They are raked over every few days until they contain only five per cent water. This stops fungus growing during shipping. They are then graded and packed into sacks ready for shipping. At this point the beans leave their country of origin. Once the beans have been fermented and dried they can be processed to produce a variety of products. The main three are:

• **Cocoa butter** – used in the manufacture of chocolate. It is also widely used in cosmetic products such as moisturizing creams and soaps.

• **Cocoa powder** – can be used as an ingredient in almost any foodstuff. For example, it is used in chocolate-flavored drinks, desserts such as ice cream and mousse, spreads and sauces, and cakes and biscuits.

• **Cocoa liquor** – used, with other ingredients, to produce chocolate. Chocolate can be a product on its own or combined with other ingredients to form confectionery products.

Orange chocolate muffins

Most of the organizations selling fair-trade items stock cocoa and chocolate, and you can also find fair-trade oranges and other fruit. Some comes from South Africa's Eastern Cape as part of the Thandi initiative. This supports the establishment of empowerment projects, where workers become co-owners of fruit farms. It is significant because it helps previously disadvantaged farmers and farming businesses enter the global economy by producing and exporting fruit that meets global requirements. As well as guaranteeing a fair price, the added 'social premium' that fair trade pays can be used to invest back into their business and community.

Makes: 12
Preparation: 15 minutes
Cooking: 20 minutes

INGREDIENTS

2 cups / 225 g flour

3 teaspoons baking powder

⅓ cup / 60 g brown sugar

¼ teaspoon salt

½ cup / 120 ml orange juice

1 teaspoon orange peel/zest

½ cup / 120 ml oil

½ teaspoon vanilla extract

¼ cup / 60 ml milk

1 egg, beaten

¾ cup / 75 g chocolate chips*

* See note p 14

Heat oven to 400°F/200°C/Gas 6

1 Combine the flour, baking powder, sugar and salt in a bowl.

2 In a second bowl, mix together the orange juice and zest, oil, vanilla, milk and egg.

3 Now, gradually pour the orange mixture into the flour bowl and mix lightly before folding in the chocolate chips.

4 Lightly grease muffin pans and fill each two-thirds full with batter. Bake for 20 minutes or so. Remove from the oven and leave in the tin for a few minutes to cool before turning out on to a rack.

Chocolate rum cake

This one-bowl cake is very good, especially with the rum. Britain's Co-operative stores stock fair-trade rum as well as many other fairly traded items, from fresh fruit and coffee to wines, fruit juice and chocolate.

Preparation: 15 minutes
Cooking: 40 minutes

Heat oven to 350°F/180°C/Gas 4

INGREDIENTS

2 cups / 225 g flour

1½ cups / 250 g brown sugar

½ cup / 60 g cocoa

2 teaspoons baking soda

1 teaspoon baking powder

½ teaspoon salt

1 cup / 220 ml oil

1 cup / 220 ml buttermilk or yogurt

2 eggs

½ cup / 120 ml hot water

¼ cup / 60 ml rum or brandy

a little icing sugar

1 Combine the flour, sugar, cocoa, baking soda, baking powder and salt in a large bowl.

2 Next, stir in the oil, buttermilk or yogurt and eggs. Add the water and mix to combine.

3 Spoon the mixture into a greased cake tin and bake for 35-40 minutes or until a skewer comes out cleanly.

4 Turn out onto rack to cool and make several holes in the cake with a skewer. Gently pour in the rum so that it seeps into the holes.

5 Leave the cake to cool completely, and sift over a little icing sugar before serving.

Shipping and processing

THE REST OF the chocolate process happens in the countries where the chocolate is produced. The beans are ground in factories often owned by big companies – sometimes chocolate companies but also those, like the US agribusiness company Cargill, which do not specialize in chocolate.

Next, the beans are cleaned, sorted, mixed with other beans, and then roasted at high temperatures. The roasting kills bacteria and loosens the shell of the bean, which is then removed when the beans are thrown against large crushing plates. The beans are next sieved and the fragments blown through wind channels, where the upward flow of air winnows the shells from the kernels.

The roasted beans are then ground in mills to produce cocoa mass (cocoa liquor). By means of a huge press, the mass is either separated into cocoa butter or powder or made into chocolate.

Great grinders

THE WESTERN EUROPE Cocoa industry grinds over a million tons of cocoa beans per year, close to a third of the world cocoa production, with the Netherlands alone accounting for 450,000 tons, which makes it the most important processor of cocoa beans in the world, followed closely by the US with 410,000 tons, Côte d'Ivoire with 285,000 and Brazil and Germany with around 200,000 apiece.

THE PROCESSING OF cocoa into chocolate is known as 'conching'. It was invented in 1897 by Rodolphe Lindt in Switzerland. This is done by a large kneading machine that also chafes, heats and aerates the batter, creating the final smoothness of the chocolate. After adding lecithin and cocoa butter, the chocolate is stored in tanks. The final process before the chocolate can be molded into bars is called tempering. This involves bringing the chocolate to just the right temperature, where the cocoa butter becomes a hard chocolate, ready for molding.

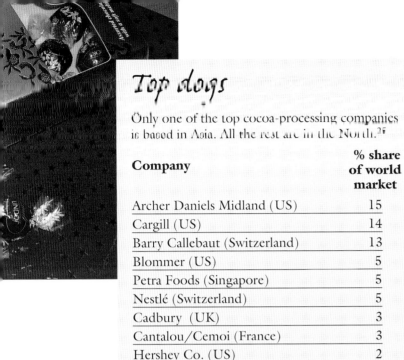

Top dogs

Only one of the top cocoa-processing companies is based in Asia. All the rest are in the North.[25]

Company	% share of world market
Archer Daniels Midland (US)	15
Cargill (US)	14
Barry Callebaut (Switzerland)	13
Blommer (US)	5
Petra Foods (Singapore)	5
Nestlé (Switzerland)	5
Cadbury (UK)	3
Cantalou/Cemoi (France)	3
Hershey Co. (US)	2
Ferrero (Italy)	2
Schwarteuer Werke (KVB) (Germany)	2
Altria/Philip Morris/KJS* (US)	2
Schokinag (Germany)	2
Mars (US)	2
Others	25
Total	**100**

*Kraft Jacobs Suchard

A chocolate glossary

Cacao the domesticated plant and all its products, before processing.

Chocolate the seeds of the cocoa plant after processing, whether liquid or solid.

Cocoa the defatted powder made from cacao.

Cocoa mass (cocoa liquor) liquid chocolate.

Cocoa butter the fat from the cacao seeds which has the texture of cream.

The terms **seed** and **bean** are used interchangeably.

Asamoah, Kate and Mamudu split open the cocoa pods and scrape out the damp white beans. These are then wrapped in plantain leaves and left out to dry and ferment in the hot West African sun.

No-bake chocolate treats

Easy and quick to make – and they taste good too. Nice to cook with the kids.

Makes 24
Preparation: 10 minutes

INGREDIENTS

1½ cups / 250 g brown sugar

½ cup / 120 ml milk

¾ cup / 170 g margarine or butter

3 tablespoons cocoa

½ teaspoon salt

3 cups / 300 g oats

1 teaspoon vanilla

1 cup desiccated coconut

1 First, put the sugar with the milk, margarine or butter, cocoa and salt in large saucepan; bring to the boil.

2 Then remove from heat and stir in the oats, vanilla and coconut. Drop teaspoonfuls onto waxed paper and leave to cool.

Orange & chocolate cookies

Tasty cookies with a zing of orange. They are best taken out of the oven when still soft. Chocolate was first used as a drink when it was introduced to Europe in the 16th century, and only in the 19th century was it produced in block form for eating.

Makes 24-30
Preparation: 15 minutes
Cooking: 15 minutes

Heat oven to 350°F/180°C/Gas 4

INGREDIENTS

¾ cup / 170 g margarine or butter

¾ cup / 175 g sugar

1½ cups / 185 g flour

2 teaspoons baking powder

2 ounces / 50 g dark chocolate*
  chopped

grated zest of 1 orange

1 tablespoon of orange juice

* See note p 14

1 Start by creaming the margarine or butter with the sugar until fluffy and light.

2 Now sift in the flour and baking powder. Add the chopped chocolate, orange zest and juice and stir to make a smooth stiff paste.

3 Roll out the paste on a lightly floured surface or press to a thickness of ½ inch/ 1 cm. Cut out rounds with a cookie cutter and place them on a greased baking sheet.

4 Now bake in the oven for about 15 minutes until the biscuits begin to color.

5 Take them out of the oven and leave to cool for at least 5 minutes to allow them to firm up; then transfer to a cooling rack.

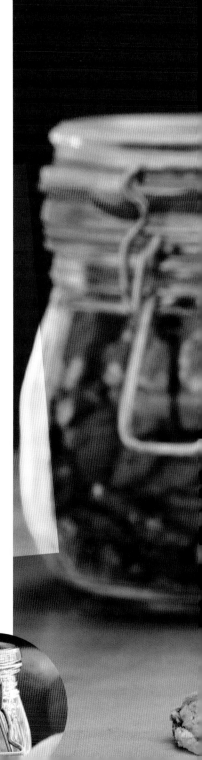

Cocoa countries

MORE THAN 35 countries grow cocoa, producing approximately 2.7 million tons of cocoa beans a year. Côte d'Ivoire is by far the most important producing country, followed by Ghana and Indonesia. Approximately 65 per cent of the world's cocoa comes from West Africa. Both the people and the countries' economies are dependent on cocoa – in Ghana, for example, cocoa accounts for 40 per cent of national income, and half the population depends on the crop in some way. There is a strange irony here; the countries that grow the chocolate – all in the South – rarely eat it, while the countries of the North that eat chocolate cannot grow it because they do not have the right climate. Chocolate is grown by poor people and eaten by the rich.

Small farmers, small prices

THERE ARE 1.5 million cocoa farms in West Africa, most of them small. Small farmers produce approximately 80 per cent of the world's cocoa. Their average annual wage is around $255 (£150).[27] If the world price drops, this can spell disaster for them and their families.

Cocoa-growing countries [26]

Country	tons
Côte d'Ivoire	1,100,000
Ghana	330,000
Indonesia	300,000
Nigeria	165,000
Brazil	160,000
Cameroon	125,000
Malaysia	100,000
Ecuador	100,000
Dominican Republic	55,000
Colombia	45,000
Mexico	40,000

A cocoa village

I MET EMILE Yabi in a little village called Biegon in Côte d'Ivoire. To get there we had to drive for hours in a bus that was not really a bus, but a lorry, overcrowded with people, filling up the roof and the back... Along the way we met people in filthy clothes returning from the fields. There was no electricity in Emile Yabi's village, only the light from small paraffin lamps. There was no running water either, so people warmed buckets of water on the fire and washed themselves. The farmers here have ten small trucks which they use to transport cocoa to the nearest town. The trucks are also used as buses – the only means of transport. In the dark we hear pigs and dogs walking around freely. People live in huts made of mud, branches and sometimes bricks. The cocoa in the chocolate we eat comes mostly from villages like this.[28]

Not on the menu

PRISCILLA AND CLIFFORD have never tasted chocolate before. Not that odd really. After all, how many children in the poor South know the same luxuries and toys that cram so much of childhood in the affluent North? The odd part of it is that Priscilla and Clifford live in a village in the Ashante region of Ghana, West Africa, which would probably not exist at all if it were not for chocolate. Camp Number One, as their village is called, owes its rather barracks-like name to a lumber camp run here in the 1950s by a British firm, Christian Brothers. Today most of the villagers' income depends upon the sale of their cocoa crops. Without cocoa there would be no money for necessities that cannot be made or grown locally, or for school fees. If they are lucky, the villagers have enough left over to pay for emergencies, a family crisis, a doctor's bill or a funeral – a significant and expensive event in Ghana. Chocolate is just not on the menu.[29]

(Left) Clifford thinks twice about opening his bar of locally-made 'Kingsbite' chocolate.

Chocolate pumpkin spice cake

If you cannot find canned pumpkin, then buy about ½ pound/225 g and cut it into small chunks for boiling. Then drain and mash. Most fair-trade outlets stock nuts and dried fruit as well as sugar and cocoa, all used here.

Preparation: 10 minutes
Cooking: 45 minutes

Heat oven to 350°F/180°C/Gas 4

INGREDIENTS

¾ cup / 170 g margarine or butter

1 cup / 175 g brown sugar

1 cup / 225 g pumpkin purée

½ teaspoon vanilla

2 eggs

1 teaspoon baking powder

½ teaspoon baking soda

½ teaspoon ground cinnamon

½ teaspoon ground ginger

¼ teaspoon ground cloves

¼ teaspoon ground nutmeg

⅓ cup / 40 g cocoa

1¼ cups / 150 g flour

½ cup / 60 g pecan or
   walnut pieces

½ cup / 50 g sultanas or raisins

salt

1 Start by melting the margarine or butter in a pan. Then remove from the heat.

2 Now mix in the sugar, pumpkin, vanilla and eggs. Sift in the baking powder and baking soda gradually, stirring to prevent lumps.

3 Next stir in the cinnamon, ginger, cloves, nutmeg, cocoa and salt. Sift in the flour and cocoa; mix well. Then put in the nuts and sultanas or raisins.

4 When this is done, grease and flour a loaf tin and then scoop the cake mix into it. Smooth the top and bake for 45 minutes. Cool in the pan on a rack for 10 minutes, and then remove from the tin and cool on the rack.

Dark chocolate brownies

Brownies should be nice and fudgy. Chocolate, sugar and nuts are all available as fair-trade items.

Makes 12-15
Preparation: 10 minutes
Cooking: 40 minutes

Heat oven to 350°F/180°C/Gas 4

INGREDIENTS

6 ounces / 150 g bittersweet chocolate

1 cup / 225 g margarine or butter

1½ cups / 250 g brown sugar

4 eggs

1 tablespoon vanilla

1 cup / 125 g flour

1 cup / 100 g walnuts, chopped

pinch salt

1 Melt the chocolate with the margarine or butter in a small bowl over a pan of boiling water. Remove from the heat and let cool a little.

2 Then whisk in the sugar together with the eggs and vanilla.

3 Next, lightly mix 1 tablespoon of the flour with the walnuts. Stir the remaining flour and salt into the sugar mixture. Now add the walnut mixture.

4 Spread the mix into a lightly greased ovenproof pan. Bake for 30-40 minutes. Remove from the oven and cut into shapes. Leave to cool and serve.

The cost of chocolate: unfair trade

'THERE WAS SOMETHING dangerous about the whole business, and the Oompa-Loompas knew it.'

ROALD DAHL *CHARLIE AND THE CHOCOLATE FACTORY*.

Chocolate chip scones

Good on their own, or with a little margarine/butter and jam. These are light, tasty small cakes and the use of chocolate chips makes them appear less rich.

Makes 8-12
Preparation: 10 minutes
Cooking: 10-20 minutes

Heat oven to 425°F/220°C/Gas 7

INGREDIENTS

3 cups / 375 g flour

¼ cup / 55 g brown sugar

4 teaspoons baking powder

¼ teaspoon salt

¾ cup / 170 g margarine or butter

3 eggs

½ cup / 120 ml milk

1 cup / 100 g chocolate chips*

1 tablespoon grated orange zest

* See note p 14

1 Using a large bowl, sift in the flour, sugar, baking powder and salt; mix well.

2 Add the margarine or butter and use a knife to cut it into the mixture to make coarse crumbs.

3 Now beat the eggs with the milk in a small bowl and then stir them into the flour mix along with the chocolate chips and orange zest until blended.

4 Next, shape the dough with lightly floured hands into a round on a floured surface. Cut with a cookie cutter into shapes and place on a greased baking sheet.

5 Bake for 10-20 minutes until golden. Cool on a wire rack.

Chocolate cinnamon flapjacks/squares

There are outlets and organizations selling fair-trade products in many countries today, and with access to the internet you can purchase items even if your local shop does not stock them.

Makes 8
Preparation: 10 minutes
Cooking: 15 minutes

INGREDIENTS

½ cup / 110 g margarine or butter

⅛ cup / 25 g brown sugar

2 tablespoons golden/table syrup

2¼ cups / 225 g oats

¼ teaspoon cinnamon

3 ounces / 75 g chocolate* broken
   into small pieces

* See note p 14

Heat oven to 350°F/180°C/Gas 4

1 Start by putting the margarine or butter, sugar and syrup into a pan and heat gently until melted.

2 Remove from the heat and stir in the oats. Add the cinnamon and chocolate pieces; stir well to distribute, and to melt the chocolate.

3 Press the mixture onto a greased sheet or shallow dish and bake for 10-15 minutes. Cool and cut into squares, leaving in the tin to cool. Finish cooling on wire rack.

Why is it so hard for a cocoa farmer?

IT IS NOT just because the crop is difficult to grow and harvest, or due to the climate, or the remoteness of the plantations, not to mention the scorpions and poisonous spiders that populate the rainforest. It is also for reasons beyond the control of any small farmer in the countries of South.

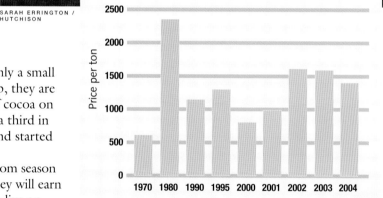

SARAH ERRINGTON / HUTCHISON

Price of cocoa beans[31] (US cents)

Future cocoa

FIRST, ALTHOUGH COCOA farmers receive only a small percentage of the final profit for their crop, they are hugely affected by the fluctuating price of cocoa on the world markets. When this crashed by a third in the 1970s, many cocoa farmers gave up and started growing other crops on their land.

But those who continued never know from season to season and from year to year whether they will earn enough for themselves and their families to live on. Farmers like Emile Yabi in Côte d'Ivoire, who owns three hectares of cocoa trees, has to supplement his income with his work as a teacher.[30]

Since 1980 the price of cocoa has dropped by almost half. The prices are set in London and New York, where traders speculate on future prices. It is a far cry from the cocoa farms of West Africa. In New York, more cocoa is bought and sold on the exchange than there is out in the real world – or ever will be.

Liberalization

Second, the liberalization of the cocoa economy has made small farmers even more dependent on the market price. The cocoa economies of West Africa were deregulated in the 1990s under pressure from the World Bank and the International Monetary Fund. Before this, cocoa was regulated by national and international agreements which protected the farmers from changes in the money they got for their crops. Now, though they pay fewer taxes, they are more vulnerable to the big swings on the world markets.

Added value

Third, while cocoa is all grown in the South it is mostly processed in the North. This is not, as is sometimes supposed, because it is highly taxed. The G8 richest countries do not tax the bean or cocoa products if they come from Africa, the Caribbean or the Pacific (ACP countries). That is good, except that of course the value comes from the processing and sale of the final chocolate – and the producing countries do not do much of this. Although some chocolate is now made in Ghana, 'Golden Tree' for example, and 'Silver Queen' in Indonesia – factors such as climate (making chocolate melt), the lack of good transport infrastructures and the fact that the capital investment is not available still make this difficult. Most of the cocoa-producing countries still just grow the beans, while foreign companies make rich pickings from the lucrative chocolate market.

Asamoah checks the pods.

SARAH ERRINGTON / HUTCHISON

Foreign firms

Finally, the International Cocoa Organization (ICCO) notes that 'the cocoa business is in the hands of a limited number of powerful international companies.' Although most cocoa is grown by small farmers who may organize themselves into co-operatives, as noted before, theirs is only a small part of the market. In Côte d'Ivoire, for example, between October 2002 and August 2003, foreign firms controlled 87 per cent of cocoa exports and local co-operatives only 8 per cent. Three major cocoa processors dominate the market and together handle over 50 per cent of the country's crop.[32]

Easy chocolate cake

This can be filled with chocolate or coffee icing (see ingredients below), or just use jam for the filling and top with melted chocolate or icing sugar.

If using coffee for the icing, try fairly traded Nicaraguan. The dark roast deepens the chocolate aroma. Some of the beans come from the consortium of fair-trade co-operatives in Nicaragua that bears the same name, Café Nica. Equal Exchange in the US first introduced this fair-trade coffee in 1986.

Preparation: 20 minutes
Cooking: 30 minutes

Heat oven to 350°F/180°C/Gas 4

INGREDIENTS

¾ cup / 170 g margarine

¾ cup / 175 g sugar

1½ cups / 175 g self-rising flour

1 teaspoon baking powder

¼ cup / 30 g cocoa

3 eggs

2 tablespoons milk

ICING:

½ cup / 110 g margarine

1 cup / 125 g icing sugar

¼ cup / 30 g cocoa or 1 teaspoon coffee

2 tablespoons boiling water

1 In a bowl, place the margarine, sugar, flour, baking powder, cocoa, eggs and milk and beat well.

2 Divide the mixture between two greased and lined cake tins. Put into the oven and bake for 30 minutes. Turn out onto a rack to cool.

3 To make the icing, put the margarine and sugar into a bowl and beat well. Mix the cocoa with boiling water and gradually add this to the mixture, stirring all the time to make a smooth mixture. Leave to cool and then use to sandwich and ice the cake.

NOTE: Instead of icing, you can fill the cake with jam. For the topping, melt some chocolate in a bowl over boiling water. When melted, pour over the cake, or alternatively just dust with icing sugar.

Chocolate sorbet

A refreshing sorbet, to end (or continue!) a meal on a sophisticated note.

Serves 4-6
Preparation: 10 minutes plus time in freezer/ice-cream maker

INGREDIENTS

1 cup / 125 g cocoa

¾ cup / 150 g sugar

2½ cups / 590 ml water

1 teaspoon vanilla

¼ teaspoon nutmeg

1 Place all the ingredients, except the vanilla and nutmeg, into a saucepan.

2 Heat gently, stirring frequently, until the mixture just begins to boil.

3 Turn off heat, and then stir in the vanilla and nutmeg. Pour into a plastic container and leave to cool. Then place in the freezer, and stir every 20 minutes or so, until it is evenly frozen; or freeze according to your ice-cream maker's instructions.

When is chocolate not chocolate?

TO EARN THE definition of 'plain' or 'dark' chocolate, a product must contain a minimum of 35 per cent total dry cocoa solids, of which 18 per cent must be cocoa butter and 14 per cent dry cocoa mass. 'Milk' chocolate must contain a minimum of 25 per cent total dry cocoa solids.

COCOA ACCOUNTS FOR an ever-smaller amount of the chocolate bar. This percentage is regulated by agreements. The average cocoa content in most of the chocolate we eat today is around 20 per cent – the higher the cocoa content, the higher the quality of the chocolate. Most countries, including the US and Russia, do not permit chocolate products to contain cheap vegetable fats which reduce cocoa-butter content (and often the dairy component) in milk chocolate.

Big bucks

THE US CHOCOLATE and confectionery industries are principal consumers of key agricultural commodities, most of which (apart from cocoa) are grown domestically.[33]

Sugar: 3 billion pounds annually or 8 million pounds a day. Confectionery and chocolate manufacturers are the second largest users of sugar in the US, most of which is domestic sugar. The value of sugar consumed in the manufacture of chocolate and non-chocolate confectionery is $800 million annually.

Milk and milk products: 653 million pounds annually or 1.8 million pounds per day. The value of dairy products consumed in the making of chocolate in 2004 was $490 million.

Peanuts: 322 million pounds of domestic peanuts annually. The chocolate and confectionery industries consume 25 per cent of the US crop.

Almonds: 43 million pounds of California almonds annually valued at $67 million.

Sweeteners: 1.7 billion pounds of corn syrup sweeteners are used annually, valued at over $205 million.

Kuapa Kokoo farmer Dora Atta with a fair-trade chocolate bar

The EU now allows up to five per cent of chocolate to consist of vegetable fats other than cocoa butter. One estimate says that this will mean that up to 200,000 tons of cocoa butter will be replaced – a possible decrease in income for cocoa producers of 12 per cent.[34] Reduced demand is also likely to push down cocoa prices. Consumer groups are concerned not only with accuracy in labeling but with the health effects of replacing a saturated fat like cocoa butter with more harmful hardened or hydrogenated fats. The Fair Trade Movement says that 'for the well-being of the Southern cocoa producers and the rights of the EU consumer, it is imperative to harmonize the market at zero per cent vegetable fats. The denomination "chocolate" must be strictly reserved for cocoa-based products not containing vegetable fats other than cocoa butter.' The name being proposed instead of chocolate for the vegetable oil candies is 'vegelate'. The name may take time to catch on...[35]

Chocolate balls

These go down well at kids' parties and of course you can talk about fair trade as they enjoy the chocolate treats. Whether they'll be listening at that moment is another matter...

Makes 12-15
Preparation: 10 minutes
Time in fridge: 1 hour

INGREDIENTS

1 cup / 175 g brown sugar

¼ cup / 30 g cocoa

½ cup / 120 ml milk

1 teaspoon vanilla

3 cups / 300 g oats

½ cup / 30 g desiccated coconut

1 Put the sugar together with the cocoa and milk in a pan. Heat gently and bring to a boil, stirring to dissolve the sugar.

2 When ready, pour it into a bowl; add the vanilla, oats and coconut and mix well.

3 Leave to cool for about 1 hour. Then take pieces of the mixture to make walnut-sized balls, and place in small paper cake cups. Store in an airtight container in single layers between waxed paper.

Chocolate pecan pie

The pecan is a species of hickory tree native to southeastern North America. The nuts have a rich, buttery flavor. They can be eaten fresh or used in cooking, particularly in desserts such as pecan pie, a traditional southern US dish. The hickory wood is also used for furniture and flooring, as well as for flavoring smoked meats.

Preparation: 15 minutes
Cooking: 35 minutes

Heat oven to 375°F/190°C/Gas 5

Ingredients

4 ounces / 100 g chocolate*

3 tablespoons margarine or butter

¾ cup / 130 g brown sugar

1 cup / 300 g golden/table syrup

3 eggs

1 teaspoon vanilla essence

pinch salt

1 cup / 100 g pecan nuts, chopped

1 unbaked 9-inch/22-cm pie shell or individual shells

* See note p 14

1 Begin by melting the chocolate with the margarine or butter in a bowl over a pan of boiling water. When melted, let it cool a little.

2 Then add the sugar, syrup, eggs, vanilla and salt and beat to blend well. Put in the pecans and mix them in also.

3 Spoon the mixture into the pie shell and cook for 35 minutes or until set. Cool on a wire rack.

Slaves to cocoa

Drissa is a teenager, and like many of his age, he traveled to Côte d'Ivoire from one of the neighboring countries, in search of work. He was offered what sounded like a good job on a cocoa farm. When he reached the isolated farm, he realized he had been tricked, but it was too late to turn back.

He and the other young men worked for long hours with no reward. At night they were locked in a small room with only a tin can as a toilet. Food was scarce and many of them suffered from exhaustion. Those who didn't work fast enough were beaten.

At times workers would try to escape but invariably they were caught. They were then tied up and whipped... They didn't know who to turn to for help.[36]

In 2001, a series of press reports in Europe and North America alleged that cocoa farmers were using child slaves. These children were alleged to have arrived in Côte d'Ivoire via a giant child-trafficking network that stretched into neighboring Mali and Burkina Faso. Several Malian children interviewed by a British film crew said they had been forced into hard labor without pay. They also said they had been physically and mentally abused. In 2001, the US State Department and the ILO followed up with reports on child slavery on Ivorian cocoa farms.

Child labor

As a result, the *Protocol for the Growing and Processing of Cocoa Beans and their Derivative Products* was signed in September 2001 between the US Congress, the international chocolate industry and several non-governmental organizations.

Research on 1,500 cocoa farms in 2002 by the International Institute of Tropical Agriculture identified 284,000 children (mostly under 14)

working in dangerous tasks such as spraying pesticides or using machetes. Some 2,500 might have been trafficked. It found that most child cocoa workers in Côte d'Ivoire do not have the opportunity to attend school because their parents are so poor and need them to work.

In 2002, the global chocolate and cocoa industry, in partnership with trade unions and NGOs, established the 'International Cocoa Initiative' to work 'towards responsible labor standards for cocoa growing, to eliminate abusive child labor practices in cocoa cultivation and processing.'

But a few years later, a survey in one Ivorian district showed that 333 children out of 500 were still working on the farms. Thirty per cent had never attended school. 'The basis of this problem is poverty,' said Amouan Assouan Acquah, who heads the national monitoring commission in Côte d'Ivoire set up to oversee the project. Child-rights advocates want chocolate to have labels saying it was not produced by child labor.

But Georges Atta Bredou, who is in charge of the monitoring project, says with so many farms and so many beans, this is near impossible. Bama Athreya, deputy director of the Washington-based International Labor Rights Fund, added that the chocolate industry had not done enough: 'They bought themselves four years of time...

The industry hasn't come through on its promises or effectively addressed the issue.'[37]

In August 2005 a lawsuit was brought against three companies, including Nestlé, over claims that they were involved in 'trafficking, torture and forced labor of children' on cocoa farms in Côte d'Ivoire. Nestlé said it supports moves to ensure cocoa is grown 'responsibly without abusive labor practices'.[38]

Biscotti with almonds, orange & chocolate

These make a nice gift – you can pack them into a decorative tin. Fairly traded almonds, sugar and chocolate can go into the mix.

Makes about 40
Preparation: 20 minutes
Cooking: 25 minutesr

INGREDIENTS

½ cup / 110 g margarine or butter

¾ cup / 150 g sugar

2 tablespoons orange peel/zest, finely grated

2 teaspoons vanilla

3 cups / 375 g flour

½ tablespoon baking powder

¼ teaspoon salt

3 eggs, beaten

1-2 tablespoons amaretto or brandy

2 cups / 200 g almond slivers, toasted

2 cups / 200 g chocolate chips*

* See note p 14

Heat oven to 350°F/180°C/Gas 4

1 In a mixing bowl, combine the margarine or butter with the sugar, orange zest and vanilla; beat until light and creamy.

2 Next, sift together the dry ingredients. Then gradually add these to the butter-sugar mixture and stir well.

3 When that is done, slowly pour in the eggs, and then the amaretto.

4 Now the almonds and chocolate chips go in; stir gently to combine.

5 Form the mixture into two flat rolls about 4 inches/10 cms wide with the length to fit your baking sheet.

6 Place the dough rolls on greased baking sheet/s and cook on the low rack in the oven until lightly golden (about 25 minutes).

7 When ready, remove them and put on a rack to cool a little. When you can handle them, cut them on the diagonal into ½-inch/1-cm slices, using a serrated knife.

8 Place the slices flat on the baking sheet/s and cook for 15-20 minutes. Cool and store in an airtight container.

Chocolate truffles

Although these are rich, dark chocolate contains more actual cocoa (which benefits the producers) – typically 71 per cent, compared with around 30 per cent in milk chocolate.

Makes 15-20
Preparation: 10 minutes
Time in fridge: 1 hour

INGREDIENTS

½ pound / 225 g dark chocolate*

¾ ounce / 20 g butter, unsalted

¼ cup / 60 ml cointreau or rum

1 tablespoon cocoa

* See note p 14

1 Break the chocolate into pieces and melt it with the butter in a basin over a pan of boiling water, stirring frequently.

2 Then, with the basin still over the boiling water, slowly add the liqueur to the mix and stir well all the time. The mixture will begin to thicken after a few minutes. Remove from the heat.

3 Line a baking sheet with wax paper. Spoon in the truffle mix and spread it evenly. Then place it in the fridge to chill for an hour or so until it is firm but still malleable.

4 Cut the mix into small squares and then squeeze each one into a ball. Roll in the cocoa before serving.

From pyramids
to plunder

'O BLESSED MONEY, which not only gives the human race a useful and delightful drink, but also prevents its possessions from yielding to infernal avarice, for it cannot be piled up or hoarded for a long time.'

PETER MARTYR D'ANGHIERA, ITALIAN HISTORIAN, 1530 *DE ORBE NOVO*.

Chocolate fruit snacks

You do not have to chop all the dried fruit (except the apricots) but it makes a smoother mixture if you do – so, best if you use a food processor or mincer. These snacks can be stored in an airtight container in the refrigerator.

Makes 10-15
Preparation: 15 minutes
Time in fridge: 2 hours/overnight

Ingredients

2 ounces / 50 g dark chocolate*

½ cup / 60 g dried apricots, finely chopped

²/₃ cup / 60 g raisins or sultanas, chopped

2 teaspoons grated orange zest/rind

For the coating (optional):

6 ounces / 150 g dark chocolate*

¼ cup / 55 g margarine or butter

* See note p 14

1 Melt the 2 oz/50 g chocolate in a bowl over a pan of boiling water.

2 When melted, remove from the heat and add the chopped fruit; combine well to make a stiff mixture.

3 Take up teaspoons of mixture and shape into balls. Place on a plate and put in the fridge to cool for 2 hours, or overnight if possible.

4 If making the coating, break the extra chocolate into pieces, place with the margarine or butter in a basin above a pan of boiling water. Stir until smooth.

5 Dip each ball of fruit in the chocolate until evenly coated. Place them on a plate and leave to set in a cool place.

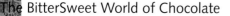

CACAHUAQUCHTL WAS NOT just any tree. It was, simply, the Tree. The seeds from its sumptuous and succulent pods were the food of the Mayan gods. In certain circumstances, when the gods looked kindly upon their people, they allowed mortals to taste their sacred food. Cacao is a Mayan name meaning 'God Food'.

This was the fourth century AD, when the Mayans held sway over the huge area between Mexico and Guatemala. They arrived around 300 BC, replacing the Olmec.

The Mayan empire reached its peak between AD 240 and 900 and included the whole of the Yucatan peninsula. The lowland areas were covered with dense forest, where the trees grew to a height of 150 feet. It was in this forest that the Tree grew and was cultivated, and here too that the Maya built their elaborate cities where images of cocoa pods were carved on the walls of temples.

Mayan civilization was sophisticated and had an extensive trade network. In El Salvador, the Mayan village of Cerén, which had been buried under three meters of volcanic ash in AD 590, was found to contain dishes full of cacao seeds. The hieroglyph for cacao is shaped like a fish. The oldest chocolate pot in the world was excavated from a royal Mayan tomb and dates back to the year 500. When it was excavated in 1984, it still contained chocolate residue under its locked lid.

Around the year 900, the Mayan civilization collapsed. No-one quite knows why, and today only ruined temples and overgrown pyramids remain in the depths of the forest to give any clues.

The Aztecs

BUT THE TREE survived. It continued to be prized by the warrior-like Aztecs who also believed that cacao had a link to the gods – this time to Quetzalcoatl (right), who brought the seeds of the Tree from the Garden of Life and gave them to humans. Quetzalcoatl (from *quetzalli*, 'precious feather', and *coatl*, 'snake') the plumed serpent, was the god of the morning and evening star and the symbol of death and resurrection. But he had boarded a raft and gone east, towards the rising of the sun. The Aztecs awaited his return.

They considered the cacao seeds to be as valuable as gold and silver. They use the beans as money; as a form of currency at a fixed market rate – you could get a rabbit for ten beans, a slave cost a hundred and a prostitute from eight to ten. It was only the inferior beans that were used to make *chocolatl*, which means 'warm drink'.

Aztec recipe for chocolatl

THE AZTECS DRIED the beans in the sun and roasted them in earthen pots. They then removed their shells and ground the kernels, or nibs, over a fire box on a stone called a *metate*. They then added a number of ingredients to the paste, which might include chili pepper, vanilla, ground maize and the *achiote* plant which gave the drink the color of blood. They made the mixture into little cakes and put these on banana leaves to cool and harden. When they wanted *chocolatl*, they broke the cakes into pieces, dropped them in water and whipped the liquid to a thick, foamy consistency. They drank it cold.[39]

IN THE 16TH century the Aztec emperor Montezuma (left) apparently saw *chocolatl* as an aphrodisiac; reputedly he drank it many times a day from a golden goblet. Taxes were paid to him in the form of cacao, and he stored huge quantities of the beans (supposedly 960 million seeds) in his palace. The drink was so precious that it was served only to nobles, warriors or merchants. It was also central to the Aztec practice of human sacrifice to the god Huitzilopochtil. Victims had to willingly give up their lives for the honor of having their hearts given to the god. The cacao pod and the human heart were seen as similar in shape. Both held precious liquids – blood and chocolate. If the victims became afraid, they were given a drink of chocolate mixed with the bloody water used to clean the sacrificial knives. A Dominican friar, Diego Durán, recorded that 'It is said that the draught had this effect on [the victim]: he became almost unconscious and forgot what he had been told. Then he returned to his usual cheerfulness and dance.'

Chocolate empires

1150-300 BC	Olmec
200 BC-900 AD	Mayan
1376-1520 AD	Aztec

Spanish plunder

WHEN HERNAN CORTÉS and his army arrived in Aztec country on 22 April 1519, the Aztecs believed he was their god Quetzalcoatl, returning from his exile. Montezuma proclaimed: 'You are the very men our fathers said would return from the land of the rising sun. You will have all that you need since this is your homeland.' Montezuma invited Cortés to his court, gave him gold and offered him a drink of the royal beverage. Bernal Diaz del Castillo, a soldier in Cortés' army, described the scene: 'From time to time they brought [Montezuma] cup-shaped vessels of pure gold, a certain drink made from cacao, and the women served this drink with great reverence.'

But it was the gold, not the cocoa, that the Spanish wanted. Cortés did not return Montezuma's hospitality. He took the king hostage and captured the capital city of Tenochtitilán, eventually winning control of the entire area. Montezuma eventually paid for his hospitality with his life, and his son was taken as a captive across the seas.

Pigs to nobles

THE SPANISH DID not like the taste of chocolate at first. One soldier wrote in his diary, it 'would be better thrown to the pigs than consumed by men'. Cortés himself, however, must have become accustomed to the taste, for he wrote to Charles I of Spain that drinking it 'builds up resistance and fights fatigue. A cup of this precious drink permits a man to walk for a whole day without food.' Before returning to Spain, Cortés had established his own cacao plantation. He took the beans back with him, along with the Aztec recipe.

In Spain, the Spanish king ordered his monks to protect the recipe and to improve on it. They added  anise, cinnamon, hazelnuts, almonds, powdered roses, orange water and sugar. They also served it hot. It was the first non-alcoholic drink to be introduced to the European continent (coffee would arrive in 1615, and tea much later).

Hernan Cortés: Developed a taste for chocolate.

The molinillo

The Spanish designed a carved wooden stick called the *molinillo* to dissolve the chocolate and make it frothy. Like the Maya, the Spanish made the paste into cakes, which made it easy to store and to use. In Mexico today, it is still possible to buy chocolate in cake form (such as Ibarra), to be crumbled into the cup.

Xocolata Amatller cocoa advertisement by Penagos in D'Aci i d'Alla, 1930. The Barcelona Amatller family made chocolate from 1797.

Dark secret

FOR NEARLY A century, chocolate remained the secret of the Spanish aristocracy. It was virtually unknown in the rest of Europe. Rumor had it that the strong taste of chocolate was useful for disguising poisons. The fanatical Charles II of Spain apparently sat sipping chocolate while watching victims of the Inquisition being put to death. Spain also controlled the supply of the bean until the late 17th century. It ran cacao plantations in the Caribbean, in Central and South America, and on an island off the coast of West Africa. In 1810 Venezuela produced half the world's supply of beans.

Eventually, however, chocolate spread to other European countries. Antonio Carletti, an Italian merchant, is thought to have taken chocolate to Italy in 1606, after he brought it back from Central America. In 1615, Anne of Austria, the daughter of King Philip of Spain, married Louis XIII of France. She introduced chocolate to the French court. In 1660 Maria Theresa of Spain married Louis XIV. She is said to have declared that 'chocolate and the King are my only passions'.

Fruit & chocolate bars

These can be made with any chocolate. The honey makes them quite sticky but delicious. According to fair-trade organization Global Exchange, the US consumes more honey than it produces. Most beekeepers feel the need to increase production by feeding their bees sugar and heating their honey for quick extraction. This in turn makes for a honey devoid of taste and nutrients. By contrast, honey produced by small growers such as the San Francisco League of Urban Gardeners comes from bees which feed only on local flora, and it is a raw honey (not heated) with a wonderful taste.

Makes 20-24
Preparation: 15 minutes
Cooking: 40-50 minutes

Heat oven to 325°F/160°C/Gas 3

INGREDIENTS

1 cup / 100 g flaked almonds

1 cup / 100 g walnuts, chopped

1½ cups / 225 g desiccated coconut

1 cup / 100 g currants or raisins

1 cup / 100 g apricots, chopped

1 tablespoon / 25 g flour

8 ounces / 200 g chocolate*

½ cup / 175 g honey

½ cup / 175 g apricot jam

* See note p 14

1 To begin, put the almonds, walnuts, coconut, raisins, apricots and flour into a large bowl and stir well.

2 Now break the chocolate into small pieces and place in another bowl over a pan of boiling water. Heat until melted and then mix with the honey and jam.

3 Stir this mixture into the dry ingredients and then transfer to a greased and lined baking tray. Use a knife to score the cut-lines.

4 Bake for 40-50 minutes or so. When ready, cut through into small squares and remove from the tin to cool on a rack.

Chocolate cinnamon fondue

Try chocolate that uses fair-trade cocoa from Kuapa Kokoo, Ghana. This co-op union of 937 village societies represents about 40,000 farmers. They currently sell about 650 tonnes of cocoa to the fair-trade market each year.

'Through Fair Trade and Kuapa we now have a lot of progress. We have good drinking water, toilet facilities and schools. Kuapa pay the farmers on time and there is no cheating. We meet every two weeks to share our problems and we are all involved in deciding how our fair trade premium is spent. Kuapa have assisted women, they ensure that women have a voice and that we are heard,' says Comfort Kwaasibea.

Serves 4-6
Preparation: 10 minutes
Cooking: 5-10 minutes

INGREDIENTS

¼ cup / 55 g margarine

8 ounces / 200 g bittersweet chocolate

¼ cup / 30 g flour

1 cup / 350 ml golden/table syrup

¼ cup / 60 ml kahlua or other liqueur

½ teaspoon cinnamon

TO DIP:

Chunks of banana, orange and apple segments, strawberries, cherries and brazil nuts.

1 First melt the margarine and chocolate together in a pan. Then sift in the flour and stir well to blend. Cook for 1 minute, stirring, and then pour in the syrup. Stir well and heat through.

2 Now remove from the heat, and blend in the liqueur and cinnamon.

3 Pour into a fondue dish and eat at once.

Drinking chocolate on the *terrasse* of a Belgian café, ca. 1900.

Chocolate houses

THE FIRST CHOCOLATE house in London was established by a Frenchman in 1657. The famous diarist, Samuel Pepys (below), wrote: 'Wake in the morning, with my head in a sad taking due to last night's drink, which I am very sorry for; so rose and went out with Mr Creed to drink our morning draught, which he did give me in chocolate to settle my stomach.' By 1700, there were nearly 2,000 chocolate houses in London alone.

In the 18th century, chocolate became immensely popular in many European countries. At this point it was still drunk mainly by the aristocracy, as it was heavily taxed and therefore expensive. The fashion was for morning chocolate, taken in bed. Chocolate also features in Mozart's *Cosi Fan Tutte*, where a maid enters carrying a chocolate pot and cups and eventually is tempted to taste it.

Poison and the Church

THERE WAS A heated dispute in the Church about whether chocolate could be taken during Lent, which revolved around a debate about whether it was a food or a drink. In 1662, Cardinal Francesco Maria Brancaccio declared that 'Drinks do not break a fast; wine, though very nourishing, does not break it in the least. The same applies to chocolate, which is undeniably nourishing but is not, for all that, a food.' In Mexico, there was a famous incident in the 17th century when the ladies of Chiapas said they could not last through a church service without their servants serving them a cup of chocolate. The bishop threatened to excommunicate them, at which point they refused to go to church. The bishop died soon after; some said that his chocolate had been poisoned. In 18th-century Italy, chocolate was the preferred drink of the Cardinals; they even had it brought in while they were electing a new Pope. Chocolate was also rumored to have disguised a poison that killed Pope Clement XIV in 1774.

New inventions

IT WAS NOT just high taxes that ensured chocolate was a luxury only the aristocracy could afford. It was also the fact that the production of chocolate remained costly and labour-intensive until well into the 18th century. Cocoa beans had to be crushed by hand or with an iron cylinder. In 1732, a Frenchman called Dubuisson invented a flat table, heated by charcoal. This meant that the cocoa beans could be ground standing up rather than kneeling on the floor. In Britain, a hydraulic press was introduced to crush the beans by machine rather than by hand. The first chocolate factories were opened in 1728 in England and in 1765 in the US. But chocolate manufacturing was then stalled by the American War of Independence, the French Revolution in 1789, and the Napoleonic Wars in Europe.

In 1828 there was progress once again. Conraad van Houten from Holland invented a press that removed cocoa butter from the cocoa, leaving a cake which could be pulverised into a powder. King William granted van Houten the patent for his invention. It was the advent of the first instant chocolate drinks.

Making chocolate in the Mixing Hall of Chocolat Guérin-Boutron, ca. 1900 in France.

Chocolate cocktail

Baileys – 'a cordial compound of coffee, chocolate, coconut, fresh cream and Irish whiskey' – works well in this.

1 serving
Preparation: 2 minutes

INGREDIENTS

Ice cubes

2 fluid ounces / 50 ml chocolate liqueur

1½ fluid ounces / 30 ml vodka or rum

a little grated chocolate

1 Crush 2 ice cubes and place in a glass.

2 Pour the chocolate liqueur and vodka or rum over the ice. Stir well and then either garnish with chocolate before serving, or strain into a chilled glass to remove the ice and then garnish with the chocolate.

Chocolate comes to the masses

AFTER THE INVENTION of instant chocolate for drinking, taxes on chocolate were lowered. For the first time, chocolate became available to ordinary people. In 1832, the *Poor Man's Guardian* ran the following advertisement: 'THEOBROMA! J Cleave begs to call the attention of his friends and the general public to the above new beverage, sold only by him at tuppence (less than 1 cent) per pint, its balsamic and nutritious properties render if peculiarly wholesome and its cheapness advantageous to the working classes.'[40]

Chocolate must have tasted like heaven to those people who were now able to drink it. Imagine the taste of chocolate in a poor person's daily diet of bread and porridge, cabbage and carrots. Even richer people in those times generally ate pretty plain fare, which would have included meat and game but still nothing sweet.

Chocolat Klaus poster by Carl Moos, ca. 1932.

Eating chocolate

IT WAS THE Swiss who invented the recipe for the chocolate we eat today. In 1819, Jean-Louis Cailler, who had trained in Italy, returned to Lake Geneva and founded a factory with a stone-grinding mill which he used to crush cocoa and sugar. In 1830 he brought out a variety of flavors. In Britain, Joseph Fry was also making eating chocolate, and in 1875 Nestlé combined chocolate with condensed milk to bring out the first milk chocolate. That same year, Rodolphe Lindt (left) invented a machine that churned the paste squeezed from cacao seeds into a smooth blend, giving it a new, mellow texture.

'Greasy as a fish-fryer's thumb'

BUT NOT EVERYONE liked chocolate. 'Some people believed it was a condensed animal jelly whose taste was imparted by various strong-smelling ingredients. Others thought it was a pie containing exotic mushrooms.' People did not like the froth (or scum) floating on top and found the drink very oily – which indeed it was before the invention of the cocoa press in 1828. One report described the chocolate served to British sailors in the nineteenth century as a drink 'as thick as soup, and as greasy as a fish-fryer's thumb'.

Coffee with rum and chocolate

Fairly traded and organically grown coffee beans can produce the highest quality taste and aroma – and benefit coffee farmers with help for education, healthcare, environmental stewardship and community development. Several organizations have campaigns to promote fair trade (see p 170). Global Exchange in the US says: 'We are building a coalition of grassroots activists, church groups, educators, coffee drinkers, and anyone who cares about social justice, to increase consumer demand for fair-trade coffee in our own neighborhoods.'

Makes 4 cups
Preparation: 5 minutes

INGREDIENTS

6 ounces / 150 g unsweetened or dark chocolate

½ teaspoon cinnamon

½ teaspoon vanilla

²/₃ cup / ¼ pint rum

2½ cups / 590 ml strong black coffee, cold

6 tablespoons double or whipping cream, lightly whipped+

sugar+

+ optional

1 Melt the chocolate in a bowl over a pan of boiling water. When it is melted, stir in the cinnamon and vanilla.

2 Now gradually add the rum and then the coffee, stirring all the time.

3 Chill in the fridge and then serve topped with the whipped cream and sugar if using.

MARY EVANS PICTURE LIBRARY

'Britannia welcomes the new cocoa' – an advertisement for Mazawattee cocoa, ca. 1890s. The old building of the Mazawattee Tea Company factory, which produced chocolate and cocoa from 1901 to 1955, still stands in London's New Cross area.

Chocolate's dark side

EUROPE'S CONSUMPTION OF chocolate was based on plantations in far-off lands. And the cacao trade had its dark side. The popularity of chocolate in Europe meant that traders were in search of new cacao plantations to supply a growing market. For a long time, Spain controlled the trade between Europe and the Americas. Other countries soon acquired their own plantations – the French in the Caribbean in 1660 and then in Brazil; the Dutch in Indonesia as early as 1560. By the 1620s the Dutch had a foothold in Curaçao, which became an important trading post for chocolate, but also for another, more sinister, trade – in slaves. The first Spanish slavers arrived in the West Indies as early as 1532, and the Portuguese brought slaves to Brazil to work on sugar plantations and then on other crops. One hundred thousand slaves a year were brought as captives from West Africa via Curaçao to work the cacao plantations. On the homeward journey the slave ships carried cacao beans and other commodities.

About 12 million people were transported to the Americas from Africa between the 16th to 18th centuries. Altogether some 25 million were uprooted from Africa, many dying on the way. This figure is comparable with the entire population of England and France at the time.

The Interesting Narrative of the Life of Olaudah Equiano or Gustavus Vassa the African (1789)

BORN IN BENIN in the late 18th century, Equiano (left) was enslaved as a young boy, but became a major voice advocating an end to slavery. His Narrative, written in 1789, immediately became a sensation.

'My father, besides many slaves, had a numerous family of which seven lived to grow up, including myself and a sister who was the only daughter. In this way I grew up till I was turned the age of 11, when an end was put to my happiness in the following manner... One day, when all our people were gone out to their works as usual and only I and my dear sister were left to mind the house, two men and a woman got over our walls, and in a moment seized us both, and without giving us time to cry out or make resistance they stopped our mouths and ran off with us into the nearest wood. Here they tied our hands and continued to carry us as far as they could till night came on, when we reached a small house where the robbers halted for refreshment and spent the night.

The next morning we left the house and continued traveling all the day. When we went to rest the following night they offered us some victuals, but we refused it, and the only comfort we had was in being in one another's arms all that night and bathing each other with our tears. But alas! We were soon deprived of even the small comfort of weeping together. The next day proved a day of greater sorrow than I had yet experienced, for my sister and I were then separated while we lay clasped in each other's arms. It was in vain that we besought them not to part us; she was torn from me and immediately carried away, while I was left in a state of distraction not to be described. I cried and grieved continually, and for several days I did not eat anything but what they forced into my mouth.'[41]

Taking out the cocoa beans from the pods in Trinidad, early 20th century.

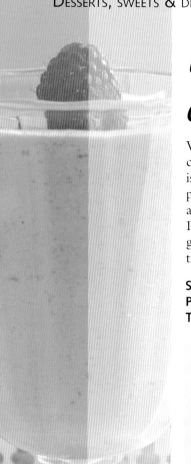

Brazil nut & chocolate mousse

Very rich and tasty – a sophisticated dessert. Brazil nuts come in very hard shells, and each cluster of 6-8 nuts is further secured in a strong outer casing (see small photo). It's interesting to speculate on how animals and humans first decided to have a go at eating them... Perhaps the outer casing cracks open as it hits the ground from the great height of the tree, or perhaps they just dry and open up in due course.

Serves 4-6
Preparation: 20 minutes
Time in fridge: 2-3 hours

Ingredients

3 ounces / 75 g bitter chocolate

water

¼ cup / 50 g sugar

4 eggs, separated

1 cup / 100 g Brazil nuts, ground or chopped finely

1 cup / 240 ml whipping cream

1 Start by melting the chocolate in a basin with 3 tablespoons of water above a pan of boiling water. Stir until the mixture is smooth.

2 Now add the sugar and mix well in to dissolve.

3 Remove the basin from the heat, and beat in the egg yolks one at a time. Then add the ground Brazils.

4 In a separate bowl, beat the cream until it is firm. Fold into the chocolate mixture.

5 Now whisk the egg whites until they form peaks and fold them into the mixture also.

6 Pour into a serving dish and chill in the fridge for 2-3 hours.

No-bake chocolate, date & nut pie

'The people of Mount Kilimanjaro are very development-oriented. As I look to the future, a better income from coffee will mean better schools, dispensaries and roads. Buying from KNCU means you get the fine quality you need, and the farmer gets the best return,' says Tobias Ndakidemi, former chair, Kilimanjaro Native Co-operative Union (KNCU). KNCU, Africa's oldest coffee co-operative, was founded in 1924 as a marketing organization for the indigenous Chagga farmers on the slopes of Mount Kilimanjaro, Africa's highest mountain. Along with all of Tanzania's coffee co-operatives, KNCU was abolished by the Government in 1976, but then reinstated in 1984. Today, KNCU has about 80,000 members from 90 local co-ops. Their smooth, mild beans are considered among the finest in Africa.

Preparation: 20 minutes
Time in fridge: 1 hour
Serves 4-6

INGREDIENTS

½ pound / 225 g dates, stones removed

4 ounces / 100 g plain chocolate

2 tablespoons margarine or butter

10 ounces / 300 g sponge cake, broken into small pieces

1 cup / 100 g nuts, chopped

1¼ cups / 300 ml whipping cream

1 tablespoon sugar

1 tablespoon cocoa

1 tablespoon instant coffee

1 First soak the dates in boiling water for 5 minutes or so. Then remove them from the water and mash.

2 Next, put the chocolate and margarine or butter in a bowl over a pan of boiling water and melt them, stirring. When melted, add the dates.

3 The sponge cake pieces and nuts go in now; mix well. Pour the mixture into a pie dish; smooth the surface, and then place in the fridge.

4 Now mix the cream, sugar, cocoa and coffee together in a pan and bring gently to the boil. Leave it to cool and then refrigerate for 1 hour.

5 When ready, whip the cream mixture until it is stiff and spread it over the pie mix.

Fair Trade

'FAIR TRADE HAS changed my life – we can rely on getting a fair price for our beans, which means I am able to stay in school... My dream is to be a scientist and to look for cures to diseases.'

RIGAYATO, FROM KUAPA KOKOO CO-OPERATIVE, GHANA.[42]

Chocolate cream dessert

Spain's contact with the New World in the 16th century made it one of the first European countries to taste cacao, as chocolate was known. But in those days chocolate was not the rich, sweet confection we know today. Mixing cocoa/cacao and sugar proved irresistible; these chocolate creams bear witness.

Makes 6
Preparation: 5 minutes
Cooking: 40 minutes

Heat oven to 300°F/180°C/Gas 4

INGREDIENTS

1 cup / 175 g brown sugar

¾ cup / 180 ml water

6 egg yolks, beaten

4 ounces / 100 g plain chocolate

1 Start by melting the sugar in the water and reduce it to a thick syrup, stirring frequently to prevent catching. Leave to cool.

2 When ready, add the mixture to the beaten egg yolks; mix well.

3 Divide between 6 small greased ovenproof dishes and then bake in the oven for 30-40 minutes or so until set. Leave the dishes to cool a bit.

4 When ready, melt the chocolate in a bowl over a pan of boiling water. Pour it over the creams and then serve.

Pancakes with chocolate sauce

If the raisins/sultanas are quite dry, soak them for 10 minutes or so in a little cold tea or orange juice. If you live in Australasia, some fair-trade organizations stock certified organic ground coffee from Café Timor, a non-profit co-op which provides an income for 17,500 coffee-growing families in the mountainous interior of Timor-Leste.

Serves 4-8
Preparation: 20 minutes
Cooking: 15 minutes

INGREDIENTS

8 pancakes*

½ cup / 50 g raisins or sultanas, softened in a little cold tea or orange juice

½ cup / 50 g ground almonds

½ cup / 100 g sugar

½ teaspoon vanilla

a little margarine or butter

oil

* FOR THE PANCAKE BATTER:

1 cup / 125 g flour

½ teaspoon salt

1 egg

¾ cup / 180 ml milk

FOR THE SAUCE:

4 ounces / 100 g cooking chocolate

1 tablespoon black coffee

½ cup / 120 ml milk

1 Start by making the pancake mix. Sift together the flour and salt in a bowl. Make a well in the center and add the egg with half of the milk. Mix well, but do not beat too much. Then pour in the remaining milk.

2 Heat a little oil in a frying pan until it is very hot. Pour in some of the batter and swirl the pan round to extend the mix over the base of the pan. Cook for a few moments and then turn or toss the pancake to brown on the other side. Repeat to use all the mixture; keep pancakes warm.

3 For the filling, mash the raisins or sultanas with the ground almonds, half the sugar and a drop of vanilla.

4 Now grease a round ovenproof dish and put one pancake in it. Cover the pancake with a layer of the nut mixture; repeat the layers until all the pancakes are used.

5 Sprinkle on a little sugar and vanilla, and dot with margarine or butter before baking in the oven for 10 minutes.

6 Make the chocolate sauce by melting the chocolate in the heated coffee and milk. Pour over the pancakes before serving.

Unfair world

THE GAP BETWEEN rich and poor in the world has increased dramatically in the last 20 years. Today, the richest 20 per cent of the world's population has 60 times the income of the poorest 20 per cent.

And the benefits of world trade are also mainly going to those who already have money to invest. Countries of the South tend to make most of their export income from cocoa, coffee, tea, sugar – what are known as 'primary commodities'.

The prices of these goods not only fluctuate from year to year (even sometimes falling below the cost of production) but also tend to rise much more slowly than the prices of the manufactured goods that the countries have to import.

And the inequalities are clear. The average family in the US or Australia spends more on chocolate in a year than the average cocoa farmer earns in the same period.

The rich get richer...

FREE TRADE BENEFITS only a few countries of the South. Of the $146 billion in private investment to developing countries in 2002, about half went to the 'emerging markets' of China/Hong Kong, India, Singapore and South Korea.[43]

'TRADE IS NEITHER inherently good nor bad,' says Hilary French, author of *Costly Tradeoffs: Reconciling Trade and the Environment*. But how it is conducted is a matter of great concern – and an unprecedented opportunity. Trade can either contribute to the process of sustainable development or undermine it. Given the rapidly accelerating destruction of the earth's natural resource base, there is no question what the choice must be.'

That choice, for many consumers, is what is known as fair trade. Fair trade already covers products from coffee and tea to handicrafts. In the face of concerns about the unfairness of the chocolate trade to cocoa farmers, chocolate has joined the ranks of products which have a fair-trade label. An independent organization, Fair Trade Labelling International, monitors and inspects producers and buyers to ensure confidence in the guarantees being offered by fair trade products. In 2005, over 800,000 producers, workers and their dependents in 50 countries benefited from being labeled fair trade. Eleven cocoa-producing organizations are certified fair trade, and fair-trade chocolate is sold in 15 countries. The object of fair trade is to give the producer a fairer wage for their labor. It:

● Guarantees farmers a stable living wage because they are paid a fair price – at present not less than $1,600 a ton whatever the world price (see chart p 156).
● Gives farmers in co-operatives control over their own production and marketing. A proportion – some $150 a ton – is reserved for community development.
● Means that women's work is properly valued and rewarded. Women are always paid for their contribution to the production process and are empowered in their organizations.
● Ensures that there is no child labor or forced labor and that people are properly paid.
● Monitors standards on a yearly basis.
● Uses ecologically sustainable methods.

Collins Adu Gyebi with pods and machete or 'cutlass', Ghana.

KAREN ROBINSON / DAY CHOCOLATE

151

Mexican chocolate drink

The Rolls-Royce of hot chocolate – very rich and creamy with an intriguing spicy flavor. Not to be squandered on the unappreciative!

A similar drink is found in Grenada. Some people there supposedly walk with a 'dancing' step which has come from 'dancing cocoa' down the generations. That refers to the way cocoa beans were polished – by people walking or dancing over them.

Serves 4
Preparation: 10 minutes
Cooking: 15 minutes

INGREDIENTS

2½ cups / 590 ml milk

1¼ cups / 300 ml cream

½ teaspoon cinnamon

½ teaspoon nutmeg

pinch ground allspice

pinch salt

2 ounces / 50 g semisweet chocolate

5 tablespoons water

2 egg yolks

1 Put the milk and cream into a bowl over a pan of hot water and bring to the boil. Add spices and salt and simmer for 10 minutes.

2 Just before serving, gently heat the chocolate and water in a small pan until the chocolate has melted.

3 Now remove from the heat and beat in the egg yolks. Then whisk in the spiced milk until the mixture thickens, and serve immediately.

Chilled chocolate drink

This is a light and pleasant drink, with the coffee creating an interesting counter-note to the cocoa and sugar. Try organic, fair-trade cane sugar grown by co-operatives of small-scale farmers in Paraguay.

Serves 4-6
Preparation: 5 minutes
Cooking: 10 minutes

INGREDIENTS

½ cup / 100 g sugar

1¼ cups / 300 ml water

½ cup / 60 g cocoa

1 teaspoon instant coffee

1 quart / 1 liter chilled milk

1 Begin by putting the sugar and water into a pan and heating gently to dissolve the sugar. Bring the mixture to the boil and cook for 5 minutes or so to make a thin syrup.

2 Take the pan from the heat and whisk in the cocoa and coffee to create a smooth paste. Put the pan back on a low heat and simmer for 3 minutes, stirring from time to time.

3 When ready, pour the mixture into a jug and place in the fridge. Just before serving, whisk in the chilled milk.

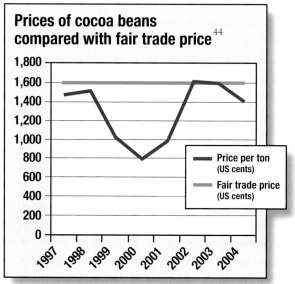

Prices of cocoa beans compared with fair trade price[44]

Price per ton (US cents)

Fair trade price (US cents)

1997 1998 1999 2000 2001 2002 2003 2004

THE MARKET FOR fair-trade chocolate is still very new, although it is growing fast. It is unlikely, despite a number of campaigns, that all chocolate will ever be fairly traded. But, as Sophi Tranchell of the Day Chocolate Company notes, fair trade 'makes other companies look at their supply chains. Our success raises the bar – if we can make a small company work, paying a fair-trade price for cocoa and still make a profit, then there is a question to answer, particularly if consumers are asking that question too. We never expected everyone to turn into fair-trade companies, but we hoped that they would improve their supply chains and do business better. It has worked in environmental terms – people have put pressure on companies and companies have had to change.'

Fair trade facts

- In the US in 2004 less than one per cent of the $13 billion chocolate market was fair trade. But sales grew by 78 per cent between 2003 and 2004 and are set to grow still further.[45]
- The business generated by fair-trade organizations in Europe and the US now accounts for an estimated $400 million, but this is just 0.01 per cent of all global trade.[46]
- In 2002 Britain's Co-operative supermarket chain, with 2,400 stores, announced that it would source all cocoa for its own brand of chocolate bars from the Kuapa Kokoo. The move should double sales of fair-trade chocolate in the UK over the next four years.
- Trade Aid in New Zealand also uses Kuapa Kokoo cocoa. Fair-trade cocoa is harvested in Belize, Bolivia, Cameroon, Costa Rica, the Dominican Republic, Ghana and Nicaragua.
- May 14 has been designated as World Fair Trade Day.[47]
- In the US in 2002, sales of organic chocolate were $13.9 million, an increase of 67.3 per cent on the previous year.

Push for Big Chocolate to use fair-trade cocoa

Companies like M&M/Mars make lots of money selling chocolate to kids, but chocolate is no treat for hundreds of thousands of children working on cocoa farms instead of going to school. Some of these kids work on their poor families' farms while others work for little or no money, even as slaves, on farms far from home. One solution is fair trade, which gives a fair price to farmers, does not allow abusive child labor, and supports the environment. Fair trade helps farmers send their kids to school, feed their families, and pay their workers. Unfortunately, big companies like M&M/Mars do not use fairly traded cocoa. You can help cocoa farmers by asking M&M/Mars for fair trade. www.globalexchange.org/campaigns

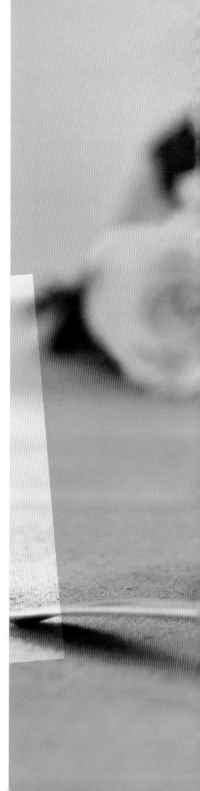

No-bake chocolate squares

Graham crackers or digestives are good for this recipe. The graham cracker originated in the US in the early 1800s by a Presbyterian minister, Sylvester Graham, as a 'health food'. They were first made solely with graham flour, a type of wholewheat. But many of today's imitations contain no graham flour at all, and are based on bleached, refined white flour, which the Revd Graham implacably opposed. His original 'Graham bread' was the centerpiece of a vegetarian diet created with the intent of suppressing carnal urges, which he believed were the source of many maladies.

Makes 16
Preparation: 10 minutes

INGREDIENTS

2 cups / 175 g semisweet cookies/
  biscuits, crushed

½ cup / 50 g hazelnuts, chopped

½ cup / 50 g raisins

⅓ cup / 75 g margarine or butter

2 tablespoons golden/table syrup

6 ounces / 150 g chocolate*

* See note p 14

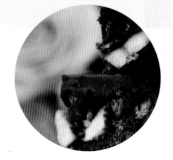

1 To begin, mix the crushed biscuits with the nuts and raisins.

2 Next, melt the margarine or butter with the syrup and then add 2 ounces/50 g of the chocolate. Heat gently and when melted stir into the cookie mixture.

3 Mix together well and then press evenly into a greased 8-inch/20-cm square tin, and set aside to cool.

4 When ready, put the remaining chocolate into a bowl over a pan of boiling water and melt it. Then pour over the cookie mixture and place in the fridge to harden. Cut into squares before removing from the tin.

Dried fruit crumble with chocolate chips

Chocolate chips were invented in the 1930s, but US giant chocolate manufacturer Hershey did not launch its first semi-sweet chocolate chips until 33 years later in 1970. Then there was no looking back, and today Hershey says 'the company has actively built its portfolio, and today is the leader in flavor variety with 15 products available.'

Serves 4
Preparation: 20 minutes plus 2 hours soaking
time if necessary for the apricots
Cooking: 45 minutes

INGREDIENTS

1 cup / 175 g dried apricots*, chopped

½ cup / 50 g sultanas or raisins

¼ cup / 25 g walnuts, chopped

½ teaspoon orange peel/ zest

juice of ½ orange

¾ cup / 100 g plain flour

1 tablespoon oats

¼ teaspoon cinnamon

⅓ cup / 75 g margarine or butter

⅓ cup / 60 g brown sugar

3 ounces / 75 g chocolate chips**

* Some dried apricots need soaking first – up to 2 hours. You can use some of the soaking liquor to put in the dish if desired.

** See note p 14

Heat oven to 350ºF/180ºC/Gas 4

1 Mix apricots, sultanas or raisins and nuts together and spoon into an ovenproof dish, together with some of the retained soaking water if using. Add the orange zest and juice.

2 Sift flour, oats and cinnamon into a bowl and rub in the margarine to make breadcrumb consistency.

3 Next, add the sugar and chocolate chips. Shake this mixture over the fruit and nut base.

4 Bake for 45 minutes until the top is golden brown. Serve with yogurt.

Percentage increase of fair-trade cocoa sales from 2002 to 2003[48]	
	% increase
Austria	22.6
Belgium	2,003.4
Canada	26.5
Denmark	0
Finland	38.5
France	596.3
Germany	1.1
Great Britain	64.0
Italy	112.5
Luxembourg	22.8
Netherlands	38.8
Norway	25.0
Sweden	4.6
Switzerland	8.4
US	4,290.5

Organic chocolate

FARMERS THAT MANAGE to pass the organic certification as well as the fair-trade one get another premium of $350 on top of the guaranteed $1,600 per ton price, though they also bear all the risks of going organic. A decade ago, organic chocolate was unheard of. But today it is becoming increasing popular. People's motivation here is more about health than equality: they are attracted by the fact that it is chemical- and GM-free.[49]

Kuapa Kokoo co-operative

'CO-OPERATIVE MEANS COMING together and caring about each other's welfare. All of the profit comes to farmers, we're not just producers. Compared to other buying agencies, Kuapa is unique,' says Anthony Bempong, President of the Ohaho Society, Kuapa Kokoo Ltd. Kuapa Kokoo ('Good farmers' in Twi, the local language) is a cocoa co-operative in Ghana that buys cocoa from its members for export and sale through the Ghana Cocoa Marketing Company. Their motto is 'pa pa paa' which means 'the best of the best of the best'. It began in 1993, after the country's internal market for cocoa was liberalized and the State no longer held the monopoly on cocoa buying. From 2,000 members it has grown to 45,000. Seventy per cent are small farmers and 30 per cent are women. Kuapa Kokoo represents about eight per cent of world sales of cocoa, with about three per cent currently going to the fair-trade market. It has five main sub-groups, which also include the Day Chocolate Company in London that produces Divine Fair-Trade Chocolate. 'Fair Trade helps to boost the morale of farmers and helps us financially. We are very proud of cocoa that we grow; it is a bridge that brings people together,' says Helena Bempong of Kuapa Kokoo.

Kuapa Kokoo Co-operative sign in Kumasi, Ghana. KK now has 45,000 members, mainly small farmers.

Vote of support

IN CANADA, LA SIEMBRA (which means the sowing or planting time in Spanish), an Ottawa-based worker-owned co-operative and Canada's largest fair-trade chocolate company, buys cocoa from the CONACADO Co-operative in the Dominican Republic, which sells on behalf of its 9,000 members directly. There are no middlemen, guaranteeing the small farmer not only a better price but also an end-of-the year profit. They depend on cocoa for 90 per cent of their income.[50] CONACADO also trains farmers to grow cocoa organically and also supplies chocolate for Cocolo, Australia's popular organic and fair-trade chocolate bar. 'The fair-trade market is a very important market for the survival of our associates,' says Isidoro de la Rosa, Executive Director of CONACADO.[51]

La Siembra also sources fair trade chocolate in the US. 'Mass market channels for fair trade are opening up,' says Jeff de Jong of La Siembra. 'We're not operating in niche markets anymore, and that's the exciting thing. And each dollar spent... acts as a vote of support for more equitable trading relationships.'[52]

Chocolate chip sponge snacks

In 1937, Ruth Wakefield invented chocolate chip cookies at the inn she ran in Massachusetts. When making cookies for guests she broke up a bar of chocolate, thinking it would melt into the other ingredients. But it did not; the little pieces remained intact – and chocolate chips were born.

Makes 12-16
Preparation: 10 minutes
Cooking: 30 minutes

INGREDIENTS

¼ cup / 55 g margarine or butter

½ cup / 100 g brown sugar

2 eggs

1¼ cups / 150 g plain flour

1 teaspoon baking powder

salt

1 cup / 100 g chocolate chips*

1 cup / 100 g sultanas, raisins or other dried fruit, chopped if necessary

* See note p 14

Heat oven to 350°F/180°C/Gas 4

1 First, cream together the margarine or butter and sugar to make a light mixture.

2 Then add the eggs, one at a time, and sift in the flour, baking powder and salt.

3 Next stir in the chocolate chips and dried fruit.

4 Grease a square baking tin. Spread the mixture evenly over the base and bake for 30 minutes. Leave to cool before cutting into bars or squares and place on a rack to cool.

Chocolate samosas

The classic Indian street food turned into a delightful dessert: chocolate mixed with curds and roasted almonds stuffed in pastry. Serve with cardamom or vanilla ice cream.

Today, at least 12 million people are in slavery throughout the world – about the same number as were enslaved in the main era of the transatlantic slave trade. 'By revitalizing the 1807 spirit, we can make the abolition of all forms of slavery, in law and in practice, a priority for each and every government in the world,' says Anti-Slavery International.

Serves 4
Preparation: 20 minutes
Cooking: 10 minutes

Heat oven to 400°F/200°C/Gas 6

INGREDIENTS

1 cup / 100 g slivered almonds

¾ cup / 180 ml cream

¾ cup / 180 ml milk

juice of 1 lemon

10 ounces / 250 g chocolate*

8 samosa pads or sheets of filo pastry**

1 tablespoon plain flour

1-2 tablespoons water

oil

* See note p 14

** If using frozen, remove from the freezer in good time to allow to thaw.

1 Roast the slivered almonds and then let them cool.

2 Bring cream and milk to the boil and add the lemon juice to curdle the mixture. Strain through a muslin cloth or a very fine sieve and squeeze out extra liquid to produce soft curds. Discard the whey.

3 Melt the chocolate in a bowl over a pan of boiling water, stirring frequently.

4 Now add the almonds and chocolate to the milk mixture and stir well.

5 Stuff the samosa pads with filling, and then seal the pads using a mix of flour and water.

6 Grease a baking sheet and cook the samosas for 5-10 minutes until golden. Allow to cool a little before serving.

Thanks for this recipe to Anti-Slavery International
www.antislavery.org

Ovidia's passion

OVIDIA ROSARIO IS a cocoa farmer in the Dominican Republic. She is 70 years old, with four children and several grandchildren.

Ovidia's passion is her community. She is one of the directors of her local women's group attending meetings twice a week. Together the women raise money for communal projects – making clothes, holding raffles and buying and selling things. They also campaign for improvements to the local school. Ovidia explains: 'You unite to make yourselves more powerful – to combine forces.' On the weekends she also finds time to visit sick neighbors in order to help with the shopping and cleaning.

Ovidia gets up at five and makes breakfast for her husband, Ovispo, and five grandchildren. She looks after the children, as their mother, her daughter, is working away from home and can't take care of them. They have breakfast at seven after which Ovispo goes to work in the cocoa farm half an hour's walk away. Ovidia spends the morning in the house, cooking, washing up and cleaning. At midday she joins her husband at the farm bringing a picnic lunch of beans, meat and rice or spaghetti, for the two of them. Afterwards they work together weeding, pruning and planting new trees. They harvest about twice a month. Ovidia and Ovispo return home around five o'clock. Ovispo feeds the animals and they prepare dinner. To relax, Ovidia watches soap operas and the news. On Saturday they attend the local farmers' group meeting and on Sunday they go to church.

They sell all of their cocoa to their farmers' association, a member of the CONACADO farmers' co-operative. Less than half reaches the fair-trade market, because as yet there is insufficient consumer demand. For this part of their crop, the farmers receive a guaranteed minimum price. The remaining cocoa is sold to the conventional market where prices have been very low, below the cost of production, for over two years. They have been earning an average of about 2,500 pesos ($86) a month which just about covers their costs and allows them living expenses.

The fair-trade price has sustained them during long periods of low market prices. Sales to this market have enabled CONACADO to set up a nursery, which supplies low-cost plants to the farmers, so they can grow most of their own food.

Perhaps the strangest thing is that this should be labeled 'fair trade'. Surely all other trade should simply be called 'unfair'?[53]

Endnotes

1 Ruth Lopez *Chocolate – the nature of indulgence*, Harry N Abrams, New York, 2002.
2 http://archive.salon.com/sex/feature/2000/12/07/sade
3 Joel Glenn Brewer *The Emperors of Chocolate: inside the secret world of Hershey and Mars*, Broadway Books, New York, 1999.
4 Ruth Lopez *Chocolate – the nature of indulgence*, Harry N Abrams, New York, 2002.
5 Judith Stone 'Lifestyles of the Rich and Creamy' *Discover* September 1988, quoted in *The Emperors of Chocolate*.
6 www.betterhealthchannel.com.au/bhcv2/bhcarticles.nsf/pages/Chocolate?OpenDocument
7 www.chocolate.org/misc/hot-chocolate.html
8 www.avma.org/careforanimals/animatedjourneys/livingwithpets/poisoninfo.asp
9 www.icco.org/questions/demand2.htm
10 www.iol.co.za/index.php?set_id=1&click_id=68&art_id=vn20050702105824895C582157
11 Figures for 2003 from www.chocolateusa.org/about-choc/facts/statistics/consumption/index.asp; www.caobisco.com
12 http://mdn.mainichi.co.jp/politics/0502/01choco.html
13 Jonathan Watts, *The Guardian* June 18, 2005
14 Joel Glenn Brewer *The Emperors of Chocolate: inside the secret world of Hershey and Mars*, Broadway Books, New York, 1999.
15 Mennonites are similar to the Amish and believe in simplicity. Many still drive a horse and cart rather than a car and wear plain clothing.
16 www.cadbury.co.uk
17 www.sustainabletimes.ca/articles/chocolate.htm
18 Figures for 2003 from www.icco.org/questions/chococomp.htm
19 Simen Saetre *The Ugly Little Chocolate Book*, Commando Publishing, Oslo, 2003.
20 www.asq.org/newsroom./news/2004/12/20041213asci_3rd_qtr.html
21 'The Cocoa Chain', *New Internationalist*, No 304 www.newint.org
22 Ruth Lopez *Chocolate – the nature of indulgence*, Harry N Abrams, New York 2002.
23 'Do we really know what pesticides are in our food?', Friends of the Earth Briefing, 2001.
24 www.pan-uk.org
25 The International Cocoa Organization's estimate for 2003/04.
26 www.eurococoa.com/cocoa/story/trade.htm
27 www.globalexchange.org/campaigns
28 Simen Saetre *The Ugly Little Chocolate Book*, Commando Publishing, Oslo, 2003.
29 The Cocoa Chain, *New Internationalist*, No 304 www.newint.org
30 Simen Saetre *The Ugly Little Chocolate Book*, Commando Publishing, Oslo, 2003.
31 www.icco.org/prices/pricesave.htm
32 www.icco.org/questions/ivory.htm
33 www.ecandy.com/candyfiles/DR_Free_trade_comments.doc
34 Simen Saetre *The Ugly Little Chocolate Book*, Commando Publishing, Oslo, 2003.
35 'The Cocoa Chain', *New Internationalist* No. 304 www.newint.org
36 www.antislavery.org/breakingthesilence/main/Activities/07_ChocolateOnMove.pdf
37 www.iol.co.za/index.php?set_id=1&click_id=68&art_id=vn20050702105824895C582157
38 www.mallenbaker.net/csr/nl/85.html
39 Joel Glenn Brewer *The Emperors of Chocolate: inside the secret world of Hershey and Mars*, Broadway Books, New York, 1999.
40 Dominique Ayral *A passion for chocolate*, Cassell and Co, 2001.
41 www.wsu.edu:8080/~wldciv/world_civ_reader/world_civ_reader_2/equiano.html
42 www.tradeaid.org.nz
43 *World Development Report 2005*, World Bank. www.worldbank.org
44 www.icco.org
45 www.globalexchange.com
46 www.fairtradefederation.com/ab_whyft.html
47 www.sustainabletimes.ca/articles/chocolate.htm
48 www.fairtrade.net/sites/products/cocoa/markets.html
49 www.organicfood.co.uk/inspiration/chocolate.html
50 www.lasiembra.com/conacado.htm
51 www.cocolo.com.au/fairtrade.html
52 www.sustainabletimes.ca/articles/chocolate.htm
53 www.fairtrade.org.uk/suppliers_growers_cocoa_ovidia.htm

Action

FAIR-TRADE CHOCOLATE COMPANIES

AUSTRALIA
The main fair-trade organic chocolate is **Cocolo**, produced by El Ceibo co-operative in Bolivia and Conocado in the Dominican Republic. **www.cocolo.com.au**

CANADA
La Siembra co-operative in Ottawa produces fair-trade organic chocolate that comes from the Conocado Co-operative in the Dominican Republic. Also sells in the US. **www.lasiembra.com**

NEW ZEALAND
Trade Aid imports and sells fair-trade chocolate from Kuapa Kokoo in Ghana. **www.tradeaid.org.nz**

UK
The Day Chocolate Company A partnership between small-scale cocoa farmers in Ghana and organizations in the UK that support fair trade. Producers of Divine and Dubble chocolate. Also sells in the US. **www.divinechocolate.com**

Green and Black's produces organic and fair-trade chocolate, but was recently sold to Cadbury's. It sources its cocoa from Belize, the Dominican Republic and Madagascar and also sells in Australia, Canada and the US. **www.greenandblacks.com**

Traidcraft Organic fair-trade chocolate grown by small farmers in the Alto Beni region of Bolivia. **www.traidcraft.co.uk**

US
Dagoba sources its organic chocolate from Conocado, and other cooperatives in Costa Rica, Ecuador and Peru. **www.dagobachocolates.com**

Equal Exchange, the oldest and largest for-profit trading company, sources its cocoa from Conocado and two farmer co-operatives in Peru and has its own brand of chocolate. **www.equalexchange.com**

CAMPAIGNS

Anti-Slavery International Information on cocoa, child labor and slavery **www.antislavery.org**

Ethical Consumer scores chocolate companies against various criteria. **www.ethiscore.org**

Global Exchange Campaigns on cocoa and other commodities **www.globalexchange.com**

Pesticides Action Network Links to national groups campaigning on pesticide use in foods, including cocoa **www.panna.org**

FAIR TRADE

The **Fair Trade Federation** The international association of fairtraders. **www.fairtradefederation.com**

Fairtrade Labelling Organizations International (FLO) is the worldwide fair-trade standards setting, certification and monitoring organization. **www.fairtrade.net**

International Federation for Alternative Trade is the global network of Fair Trade Organizations, working to improve the livelihoods and well-being of disadvantaged producers and speaking out for greater justice in world trade. **www.ifat.org**

The Fair Trade Association of Australia and New Zealand **www.fta.org.au**

PRODUCERS

Conacado is a co-operative producer group in the Dominican Republic with a membership of 9,000 small-scale cocoa farmers. **www.conacado.com** (Spanish) or via **www.lasiembra.com/conacado**

Kuapa Kokoo is a co-operative of over 40,000 small-scale cocoa farmers in Ghana, West Africa who own a third share of The Day Chocolate Company and produce the beans for Divine and Dubble. **www.kuapakokoo.com**

THE CHOCOLATE INDUSTRY

You can look at individual companies' websites. The **International Cocoa Organization www.icco.org** has lots of facts and figures on the industry and on cocoa in general.

FURTHER READING

A passion for chocolate. Dominique Ayral, Cassell and Co, 2001. A handy little book with lots of facts and figures.

The Emperors of Chocolate: inside the secret world of Hershey and Mars. Joel Glenn Brewer, Broadway Books, New York, 1999. Fascinating details on the chocolate empires.

Chocolate – the nature of indulgence. Ruth Lopez, Harry N Abrams, New York, 2002. A glossy book with lots of photos and a history of cocoa.

The Ugly Little Chocolate Book. Simen Saetre, Commando Publishing, Oslo, 2003. The darker side of the chocolate trade.

The Cocoa Chain, **New Internationalist** No. 304. A journey to Kuapa Kokoo and back with Asamoah, a cocoa farmer. **www.newint.org**

What YOU can do!

- When buying chocolate, look for a brand with high cocoa content (more cocoa means higher quality and – at least potentially – more farm income).

- Encourage your stores or supermarkets to carry chocolate brands that are certified as being fair trade or slavery-free.

- Look out for chocolate that carries a 'fair-trade' label or the mark of a similar socially responsible producer.

- Contact organizations on opposite page for campaigns and information.

KAREN ROBINSON / DAY CHOCOLATE

Subject Index

173

Index of recipes and main ingredients

About the authors

Nikki van der Gaag is a freelance writer, editor and evaluator on development issues. Prior to this she was editorial director at the Panos Institute and co-editor with the **New Internationalist**. Normally she specializes in gender, poverty, human rights and refugees, but she is always partial to a bit of fair-trade chocolate!

Troth Wells joined the **NI** in 1972, helping to launch the **New Internationalist** magazine and build up its subscriber base. She is now the Publications Editor and has produced six books on food and cooking, including *The World in Your Kitchen* (1993), *The Spices of Life* (1996) and *The World of Street Food* (2005).

About the New Internationalist

The **New Internationalist (NI)** is a not-for-profit co-operative based in Oxford, UK, with associated offices in Adelaide, Australia; Toronto, Canada; Christchurch, New Zealand/ Aotearoa; and Dublin, Ireland. Founded in 1972 with the backing of Oxfam and Christian Aid, the **NI** has been fully independent for many years. It publishes the **New Internationalist** magazine, with 75,000 subscribers worldwide, which reports on global issues, focussing on the unjust relationship between rich and poor worlds. The **NI** also produces publications including the One World Calendar, the *No-Nonsense Guide* series to topical political issues; food books such as *The World of Street Food*, and photo books including *Our Fragile World*. **www.newint.org**